D1329781

THE SHORTEST PENCIL
BY GLENN MARSH, MD

CHICAGO SPECTRUM PRESS
LOUISVILLE, KENTUCKY 40207

CHICAGO SPECTRUM PRESS
4824 BROWNSBORO CENTER
LOUISVILLE, KENTUCKY 40207
502-899-1919

PREFACE

As I sat outlining some rather lengthy instructions to an elderly patient, I glanced at her almost equally elderly brother, who had accompanied her, as he was writing hurriedly to keep up with me. I paused, he finished writing, looked at me, and matter of factly stated, "Doc, I learned a long time ago that the shortest pencil is better than the longest memory,"—hence the title of this book. As was usual, I learned more from my patients than they from me.

DEDICATION

This compilation of anecdotes, stories, recollection of feelings, insights, quotes, and happenings is dedicated first of all to Judy Love—my buddy, best friend, sweetheart, and wife. She has brought out the best in me and is the source of great joy in my life. Her parents, Ruth and Berl Hopkins are now my family, filling in for my own mother and father, now deceased, who had vision and faith enough to take them from a sharecropper cotton patch to Auburn, Alabama where their three children, all sons, received college degrees and all received earned doctorate degrees. Secondly, I dedicate this to my patients who numbered roughly one quarter million. They trusted, inspired, helped, shared with, thanked, and supported my family and me, and twelve years after retirement, I'm still getting an occasional call requesting an appointment. Thank you from the bottom of my heart!

ACKNOWLEDGMENT

Judy Love planted the seed for this book as she heard me reminiscence, fondly relating story after story of my youth, school days, college, graduate school, medical school, army service, and medical practice. Unhappily, and unwisely, I kept no journal, but blessed with a good memory, I have recalled enough significant and insignificant information to paint a word picture so that the reader may judge for himself the worth of this endeavor.

Some listeners to these true stories indicated that if they were ever compiled in a book, they would like a copy. I thank them for their encouragement.

Special thanks are due
- Carl Hurley, EdD, LLD premier humorist of Kentucky, speaker and author of *We Weren't Poor–We Just Didn't Have Any Money*, for his objective assessment of this book and his gracious encouragement and support. Knowing him has enriched my life.
- Carolyn Ellis Lipscomb for Lipscomb family photos and permission to use same. Carolyn also made helpful suggestions relative to the publishing process and her book *The Widow's Might* was an excellent model to follow.
- Leon Marsh, PhD for supplying Marsh family photos and critique, especially pertaining to dates and identification of subjects in photos.
- Robert Holman, MD, author of *The Black Bag*, for critique, especially in the medical related sections of the book.
- Patsy Holman for critique of the manuscript.

– Shelby Kinkead, JD for his critique of the book and his legal opinion.

– Auburn University for permission to quote *The Auburn Creed* by Dr. George Petrie.

– Dorothy Kavka of Evanston Publishing, Inc for her expertise, encompassing her artistic abilities in the design of the dust jacket and her valuable editorial advice. She guided with a firm hand, yet sympathetic attitude, thus, smoothing the path to publishing.

– John Hockersmith for furnishing a key photograph and for his encouragement.

– Tom Barnett Photography for permission to use photographs.

CONTENTS

YOUTH AND ELEMENTARY SCHOOL

Birth

I was born September 22, 1929 on a farm near Arab, Marshall County, Alabama. I was the third son born to Albert G. Marsh (born April 18, 1894; died May 4, 1960) and Ethel Lee Cox Marsh (born June 6, 1896; died October 7, 1985). My second older brother, Leon, relates his memory of the day of my birth, telling how our father took him, along with our older brother, Ralph, to stay with Cora Lee and Lawrence Cox, an aunt and uncle, during the time of my birth. After the event, as Leon further tells, when Daddy picked up the two of them, they stopped by to tell my grandma Cox about my birth stating, "We have three sons," to which Grandma Cox misinterpreting in a state of excitement, responded saying, "Ethel had triplets!"

Memories of Early Days
Sharecroppers in Arab

Mother and Daddy were poor sharecroppers on a farm near Arab, Alabama in the depression years and raised cotton as the sole money crop. I remember that we had a car, but the Great Depression's effects precluded the buying of gas, so whenever we went anywhere, it was almost always by mules and wagon. All the farm labor was, of course, by hand with chopping and hoeing cotton, harvesting corn, and putting up fodder as feed for the mules. We had a smokehouse where hams were cured, a well where we obtained our water, and a yard, which was bare

Grandma Sallie Cox, Glenn, and cousin, Gene Cox. Picture taken on Beaman Hawk farm, located on Arab-Guntersville Road. I remember the sycamore tree and especially the mailbox. Tom Wright, brother of my uncle Joe Wright, hit and knocked down this mailbox as he drove out into the road. He yelled as he drove away, "I'll be back tomorrow and fix it." He was very ill and died of pneumonia the following day. Picture circa 1934, courtesy of Dr. Leon Marsh.

of grass and swept with a broom made of tied together brush. I had three possessions of which I was very possessive, a dog–mostly Collie–named Tip, a tricycle, and my plate, which was really a bowl with more or less vertical sides, sort of like a dog dish. Seeing education as the way out of poverty, my folks decided to move to Auburn, Alabama in order that their three children would get a good and complete education. I was only five years old at this time, but I remember being concerned that I would be allowed to move all three treasures. So on a hired rickety farm truck in the fall of 1935, all our possessions were duly loaded and transported to that far away place (186 miles), which seemed to me as a foreign country.

My brother says that after paying the truck owner/driver, also paying the first month's rent, and buying staples such as flour, the family fortune amounted to a grand total of two dollars and fifty- seven cents of which he says the seven cents were his. This sum represented the net sharecropping proceeds from farming 19 years on seven different farms.

Marsh brothers, (L to R) Leon, Glenn, and Ralph on Wire Road, Auburn, Alabama, 1937

Glenn and pets, Wire Road farm, Auburn, Alabama, 1937

After my family settled in Auburn, my brother Ralph entered Alabama Polytechnic Institute (now Auburn University) majoring in Veterinary Medicine, brother Leon entered high school, and I began elementary or as called in those days grammar school. I have a picture of Miss Frances Duggar's first grade class in which most of the class are barefoot including many girls.

A short time after our move, I was quite ill, with a high fever. On this particular day, my father came in from work, wearing what today is called a chore coat. In those days, it was called a jumper. Made of denim, it had two big side pockets and a zippered upper chest pocket in which my father carried his dollar watch, Ingraham brand. It really did cost just a dollar and kept reasonably good time, but had a loud tick that sounded like an alarm clock, in that it could be heard across the room. On this occasion, one of the side pockets of his coat held a treasure, a six-and-one-half-ounce bottle of Coca Cola, my first nectar of the gods, and I was hooked for life. I can remember how good, how cold, and how soothing to my fever. To this day, it remains, by a wide margin, my favorite soft drink of all time.

Teachers in those days, other than Miss Duggar, were Mrs. Lane, second grade; Mrs. Martin, third grade; Miss Annie Bell Taylor, fourth grade; Miss Helen Williams, fifth grade; and Mrs. Murphy, sixth grade. After sixth grade, we were promoted to junior high school for grades seven through nine, then senior high school for grades ten through twelve. We had various teachers in both junior and senior high school, but my all-time favorite pre-college teacher was Miss Lucille Rhodes, THE English teacher.

A Different Language

When I was in the second grade, Mrs. Lane, one morning having seen Lynwood Story enter her room, and then noticing, a short time later, that he was not at his desk, asked, "Where is Lynwood?"

A classmate replied, "He's in the cloak room eating goober peas."

Now, tell me, when was the last time (or have you ever) heard peanuts referred to as goober peas?

Two Nickels

It was our custom to go to Opelika, Alabama, seven miles from Auburn, for shopping on a Saturday afternoon about once a month. This was in 1937 and the depression was far from over. My mother gave me a nickel, and having seen this particular lead toy soldier many times before, I hastened to the 5 & 10 cent store to make my purchase. When I returned to the car, I was playing with my treasure in the back seat when this terribly poor family came down the sidewalk. I can remember the remorse/guilt I felt for having spent my nickel so selfishly.

At about that same time, give or take a year or two, friends visiting with my mother and daddy gave me a nickel as they left. I liked having the feel of money in my pocket. But a nickel in the pocket of an active seven-year-old is not a substitute for a bank. I lost my nickel and spent all Sunday afternoon looking for it to no avail. I went from rich to busted in one-half day.

Learning One's Right from One's Left

In a time without electricity, running water, or close neighbors, we often visited as a form of entertainment on Sunday afternoons. There were no refrigerated soft drinks or goodies to be served, but in the summertime, there were watermelons to be cut, but when fruit was not in season, the host would draw a bucket of fresh well water, pour it into another bucket, which was then passed around. Guests were served first, host family second, and children last. Early on, I noticed that most people drank out of the same side of the common dipper (right handed) and few, if any, the other side. After observing the snaggle-toothed people with the snuff and chewing tobacco stained corners of their mouths, I became left handed, if only for drinking-water-from-dipper purposes. Yuuk!

"That's Just the Way I Like It"

The second year after our moving to Auburn, my father rented a worn-out farm on Wire Road. The farmhouse was a cold, heated-by-fireplaces affair, with no indoor plumbing. Money was scarce in 1936 and 1937, so my parents rented a room to two or three college students – I believe it was three – who shared this one room. Electricity was brought in about this time, and I suppose their cooking was by hot plate. As their room was separated from ours by a thin, un-insulated wall, and as we spent most of our time in the kitchen, the only warm room because of the wood cook stove, we heard their conversation almost as clearly had they been in our presence. We learned that their job assignments were dictated by complaint. The cook remained the cook, until someone complained about the cooking. The complainer then became the cook.

I remember this episode: at supper one of the trio said, "Wow, these beans sure are salty!" And quickly remembering the penalty for complaining about the cooking, hastily added, "And that's just the way I like 'em!"

JIM ED BUTLER

One of the three students sharing the room was a native Alabamian enrolled in engineering. I remember nothing of the other two. Jim Ed Butler was the one who stood out. For instance, he stretched a steel cable between two trees in the yard and practiced walking this cable to enhance his coordination resulting in grooves being worn in the soles of his shoes as he performed this feat. Once, I forgot about the cable, as seven year olds are apt to do, and was riding my tricycle at dusk when the cable caught me just under the chin, giving me an unexpected back flip when all but my head passed underneath.

Jim Ed, who was a P-38 fighter pilot in WW II in North Africa, was reported missing in action. Neither his body nor aircraft was ever found. His younger brother Gilbert was at A. P. I. during my student days there, and when I saw him and his wife at the Baptist Student Union reunion several years ago, Gilbert told me of Jim Ed's continuing legacy. When Jim Ed was declared dead, the National Service Life Insurance policy funds, paid his parents, were donated to help build a church, the ministry of which led to Jim Ed's and Gilbert's father's becoming a Christian.

His indomitable spirit lives on.

GROWING UP IN THE SEGREGATED SOUTH

I grew up in the segregated South. There were no black people in Arab, Alabama, the town where I was born, and I think not many in Guntersville, the county seat. There were, however, many in Lee County where we moved in 1935. Here I learned to appreciate the black dialect, especially as it was reflected in songs and black sayings which I found most apropos.

Living on a farm in 1937, I was privileged to hear the singing of black farm workers as they picked cotton. I remember the dozen or so pickers moving in a flowing line across the field with first one, then another singing the solo parts of songs I do not recall having heard before, with all workers joining in chorus. The music had a haunting, plaintive, albeit sad quality, the sound of which I do not recall hearing again until years later on a Sunday evening when I heard the same kind of music emanating from a black church, a block or so off the usual route from Emory to Grady Hospital. After locating this church, we would, on occasion, park near the church and with the aid of open windows of summertime, sit in the car with the children, and listen intently. I suppose from these and other experiences, I have gotten the idea that all black people are born singers.

When I was six or seven, a black lady named Mollie helped Mother on occasion and one day, in my child's mind, I thought I had figured out the difference in the races, telling her that white people told whites lies and black people told black lies.

As an interesting side note, when I opened my office in 1968, I had quite a few black patients early on, then more as some of the black physicians, especially Dr. Hunter, referred to me, certainly more black patients percentage-wise than the percentage of this ethnic group in the general population. As a matter of fact, the most endearing compliment of all my years of practice came from one of my black patients as I have related in the vignette, "Doc, I's been watchin' you."

TOUGH MAN

When I was a pre-teenager growing up in Auburn, Alabama, Mrs. Chrietzberg was a neighbor on North Ross Street where she ran a boarding house, primarily for college students.

I remember she had a pomegranate bush near the sidewalk, and as I passed her home twice daily, enroute to school and back home again, I watched the growth and maturing of the fruit. When the fruit appeared fully ripe, I succumbed to temptation and misappropriated one. Having read favorable reviews of this supposed delicacy in the Bible, I could hardly wait to peel it and enjoy the fruit of my ill-gotten gain.

What a disappointment. It was mostly seeds with a thin coating of fruit pulp and this so sour as to defy description. Don't try it. You won't like it.

Mrs. Chrietzberg had a boarder named Euless Light from Arab, Alabama. He was a robust, strapping young man who had enrolled in Auburn as a student athlete and was to be a football player.

He had been living at the boarding house for about three or four days when upon meeting Mrs. Chrietzberg in the hallway, asked, "Is thar air sank around hyar whar a feller could warsh his hands?" She wondered if this were the first attempt at personal hygiene since he had moved there.

Hazing of undergraduate students was common in those days and freshmen, called *rats* were "encouraged" by upperclassman to wear a blue and orange (Auburn's colors) baseball cap look alike referred to as rat caps. While hazing was officially frowned upon, freshmen were often hazed by paddling as part of the campus scene. Traditionally, true freshman were to eschew passing through the main entrance to the college across the street from Toomer's Corner and were to walk around, not through, the gate. A group of hazers, mostly football players, came to the Chrietzberg home and finding Light's room, attempted to take him outside to administer the paddling, but he held fast to his iron bedstead precluding his bodily removal. Unwilling to admit they had been outfoxed by this Brindlee Mountain boy, they lighted matches which they held close to his hands. In spite of the pain, he held on, and after this unsuccessful effort to separate the potential victim from the bed, the hazers gave up.

As result of this experience, Light left school forthwith and the next, and last event of which I have knowledge, occurred when Light, just a few years later, was in combat in WW II in the South Pacific. The officer in charge asked for a volunteer to string wire for necessary field communications. This involved carrying a heavy roll of wire, unrolling it as he traveled through enemy-held areas of the jungle. Light's only request was that he be allowed to proceed barefoot on his mission, which was expeditiously accomplished.

Tough man, indeed.

CHRISTMAS PAST

When I was a pre-teen, Christmas in Alabama was very different insofar as celebration of this holiday is concerned than now, at least, in the northern part of Alabama around Marshall County. The celebration was a composite of Christmas, the Fourth of July, and Halloween as there were fireworks and firecrackers for both children and adults, and a version of trick or treaters, always adults, referred to as *serenaders*. These adult serenaders would come by after supper, not singing, but dressed in makeshift costumes. The women might be wearing their husband's clothes and shoes, for example. The object was for the family to try to guess who the disguised visitors were. If the family being visited could not guess the identity, then the serenaders were rewarded with a gift, usually Christmas goodies. Incidentally, the previous version of the musical drama *The Stephen Foster Story* in Bardstown, Kentucky had a Christmas scene with serenaders. As far as I know, this tradition is no longer practiced.

BEST SEAT IN THE HOUSE

When I was ten years of age, the movie, *Gone with the Wind* was released with a premiere in Atlanta. Soon it was shown in

Auburn, Alabama and at that time, I delivered, from house to house in certain parts of town, programs, previews of coming attractions, for the Tiger Theater. As payment for doing this, I was allowed admission to all the picture shows, now called movies, which I cared to see, but on this occasion, there was a directive by the theater ownership that no passes were to be issued for *Gone With the Wind*. However, the manager, Mr. Gus Coats stashed me backstage, started the movie, then led me to my seat. What a treat. A great three-and-one-half hour plus spectacular, and it is to this day my all time favorite movie. Thank you, Mr. Coats.

Alas, the Tiger Theater and Mr. Gus Coats are no more.

LOOK OUT FOR THE GOOD GUY

I was always looking for ways, honest, of course, to make money and an opportunity in the form of cutting stencils came along. Cutting stencils in those days meant just that. The message was outlined on the sheet of stencil material by tracing the outline of the letters of a completed stencil. The letters were then cut out using a single-edged razor blade (expensive) or in my case, my trusty pocketknife. There were four messages and I still remember two of them which were "Careless Matches Aid The Axis" and "Help Prevent Forest Fires."

A friend (?) and I agreed to share the job at so much per completed stencil, and while I do not remember the number to be done, I do remember that my friend's mother, the preacher's wife, picked up the master stencils and the stock of material for the stencils. I also remember that my friend was through with his stencils long before I was. Is it not reasonable to assume his mother intentionally gave him the shorter set?

SWEETS FOR THE SWEET

When I was a pre-teenager, like most of my friends, I was especially fond of sweets, such as Kool-aid, candy, cookies, you name it. One especially delectable item, which was always in short supply at our home, was maraschino cherries. They were only in evidence on top of a dollop of salad dressing, on top of a Bartlett pear half, on top of a half leaf of lettuce, but only when we had guests. Since I was expected to consume all of the salad, not just the top story, my appetite for cherries was never assuaged. Staley Fincher, a classmate, in discussing this sorry state of affairs with me, agreed to form a plan to share jointly a maraschino cherry feast. Money was always in short supply too, so we needed a means of raising cash. We walked the railroad tracks and gathered enough discarded pop bottles (twenty-two, redeemed at one cent each) to buy a small bottle of the desired cherries from Mr. Jerry Williams, who ran the neighborhood grocery, a one-man operation. After the transaction was successfully completed, we repaired to the shade of a friendly oak tree in Staley's front yard. Each of us, armed with a toothpick, took turns spearing the delectable treat and when finished with the fruit, we passed the bottle, taking small sips of the very sweet juice until all was gone.

About fifteen to twenty minutes had passed when I noticed a great difference in the surroundings to which I was accustomed. Things seemed unaccountably a great way off when I knew well they had not been transplanted. Maybe they weren't that far away, but they appeared very small, like looking through binoculars the wrong way. Things also seemed canted; it was like being in a land where everything was in miniature and all the buildings were Leaning Towers of Pisa. With my head swimming, things took on something of a greenish cast. I hurriedly headed for home as the wave of nausea overtook me. Fortunately, I arrived there and the bathroom just in time. I was to experience something on this order again when I smoked a cigar for the first time. I still don't care for maraschino cherries (or cigars), and even when served just one, push it aside as memories of the past are still strong, bringing back more than a hint of that queasy feeling.

The experience may be summarized by saying that I was an alimentary canal without responsibility at either end.

High School
The Botanist

As a teenager I had several interests though the most intense by far was the construction and flying of model airplanes. Another close second was the study of medicines, especially those derived from plants. Somewhere I had read that the common tomato was a member of the *deadly nightshade* (solanaceae) family and that the common Jimson or Jamestown weed was also. I reasoned that if so, one should be able to graft the tomato with its weak stem structure onto the strong Jimson weed. I tried it, and it worked with tomatoes hanging like apples from that vigorous Jimson weed. I don't recall the taste of the tomatoes so grown, but I recall the startled neighbors coming by to see what Glenn had done.

Later as a pharmacy student at Auburn, I remember Professor George Hargreaves telling us during a lecture that there was a statue in South America, dedicated to the first person using the tomato as food. Previously, it had been considered inedible, as almost all members of the deadly nightshade family are poisonous. Known as *Love Apple*, it was not generally accepted as a food until the early 1800's.

Model Airplane Adventures

As previously noted, my main interest during high school was model airplane building and flying. Herbert Hathcock and I spent many hours enjoying this hobby. We would use the playground at the school for U-control, wherein the plane was flown by the operator in an around-and-around manner controlled by wires about fifty feet long from plane to operator. Herbert was fond of this, but I preferred free flight, wherein the plane's engine was started and allowed about twelve to fifteen seconds of fuel and launched. Open fields or land surrounding the airport were required for this. Jimmy Dick, a Navy pilot killed in a mid-air collision during the Korean War, was an early model airplane builder in Auburn, as was Martin Beck. Martin and I also shared some good times flying gliders and U-control models on the high school playground, which was immediately behind his home.

On one memorable occasion in our high school days, Herbert and I caught a Greyhound bus about 4:30 a.m. for Marietta, Georgia to attend a model airplane contest. He lived two and a half very long blocks away, and as I emerged from my home in darkness, I walked toward his home to meet him. As I saw him coming, I was suddenly struck with a moment of mischievous inspiration. I knelt down behind a hedge alongside the walk, and as he came abreast, I came up lunging toward him from behind the hedge; he immediately became airborne toward the center of the street. I think he remembers that as much as the long bus ride and the eventful day.

Mr. Guthrey

Mr. M. D. Guthrey was a wonderful person and teacher who taught chemistry and physics at Auburn High School, Lee County High School until about 1960, when its name was changed. He was quite religious and would work moral precepts into his teaching in those halcyon days. He also wielded a mean meter stick, which he used to make his point during lectures, and if the students dozed off, was known to bring it down sharply striking the surface of the laboratory desk with a resultant loud bang.

Mrs. Guthrey had given him an expensive watch for Christmas one year, and he took it off as usual before his lecture, placing it on the laboratory desk – he forgot exactly where – and as you might imagine, came down with that meter stick hitting it dead center.

No more watch.

MISS LUCILLE RHODES

My favorite high school teacher, hands down, was Miss Rhodes. She taught English with verve, class, and enthusiasm, while demanding the students' best efforts.

My most vivid memories of Miss Rhodes are:

- Her tossing upon my desk with disdain and without grade, a theme I'd written, as she said, "You can do better than this. Write it again."
- Her pointing a bony forefinger at me as she said, "Boy, if you don't learn this English, I will grind your bones to make my bread," and I believed her.
- Her reading Robert Burns' poetry with her idea of a Scottish accent.
- Her reading "The Outcasts of Poker Flat" by Bret Harte, and parroting the only good thing that anyone could say about the deceased tin horn gambler when he was being buried in boot hill —"Well, he war a good speller." After reading that line she would cackle with a raucous, unfeminine laugh that delighted us all.

One day Miss Rhodes asked the class a question; no one knew the answer. She asked it again. Still no answer, but then a voice from the heavens answered correctly. For a moment, I considered that maybe God had answered. With her commanding presence, she could have known Him on a first name basis.

No, it was only a workman, one of Miss Rhodes' former students, on a scaffold outside the building above window level.

THE PROFESSOR BECK STORY

Professor Martin Luther Beck was my sociology teacher in high school. I related well to him and remember well his statement, "No matter where in the world one goes, there will be found four American products – Standard Oil, Singer Sewing Machine, Ford, and Coca-Cola."

While in the combat area of Korea, I noted ancient battered Ford cars and trucks, Singer pedal-operated sewing machines, but no Standard Oil or Coca-Cola. Considering the circumstances, my seeing two of the four proved his point.

That morning in 1944 or 1945 when I arrived at Lee County High School, I remember as the saddest day of the war for the students and faculty. Martin, son of Professor and Mrs. Beck, had been reported missing in action, but was later reported as a prisoner of war by the Germans. In my memory, it seems as though, in a trance, we went through the motions of being at school that day with a deep, deep pall of anxiety and grief – almost palpable. As I had two brothers overseas, this event brought me face to face with the reality of war.

Thankfully, Martin returned home safely, and I spent many pleasurable hours with him sharing our mutual interest in model airplanes. He is now married to Mary Williams, widow of B.B. Williams, PhD.

THE RAPE OF THE LOCK – AUBURN STYLE
. . . WITH APOLOGY TO ALEXANDER POPE,
ENGLISH POET (1688-1744).

In Greece, it is not uncommon to see men with a string of beads called worry beads which come out of their pockets at times of stress, so that they may be fondled or stroked, so as to relieve the tension of the moment. We, of course, have our own equivalent such as twisting a lock of hair or biting our nails. A student (C.R.M.), who sat in front of me in math class at Lee County High School had his own permanently attached worry wart, actually, mole. It was strategically located below the collar line at the left posterior base of his neck. During an exam, he would launch into answering the problems, but when he would hit a snag, he would place his pencil in the slot at the front of his desk, reach back with his left hand, pushing his collar out of the way and finding his worry mole would caress it, and as a part of this tension relieving exercise, would also isolate the

Ralph Marsh and Leon Marsh at home on leave, WW II;
160 Ross Street; Auburn, Alabama, circa 1943

two long hairs growing from the mole, and with his thumb and forefinger compressing the hairs slide these two fingers down the length of the hair. This motion was repeated over and over while his mind was fixed on the problem. Coming to a decision in reference to this, he would again pick up his pencil and resume the solution of the math problem.

Having witnessed the above sequence several times, I decided to modify the mole. I sneaked my mother's small sewing scissors to class shortly before the next exam and in class as he leant forward, exposing the mole and two hairs, I, with the deft movement of a surgeon, snipped off the two hairs close to the surface of the mole. I eagerly awaited the upcoming exam, not usual for me. Well, he whizzed through the first few minutes of the exam, but about the fourth or fifth problem, he hit a snag and as before, parked his pencil, reached for old faithful mole, found it easily, but when he attempted to stroke the two hairs, there was an immediate reaction. Panic is an alternate description. In something approaching a seizure, his right hand assisted his left in attempting to find the missing hairs, and in being unable to do so, he repeatedly slapped both sides of his neck individually and in unison in a frenzied effort to find the missing hairs. Witnessing all of this, I was in a near convulsive state suppressing my pent-up laughter. I succeeded and it was with great effort that at our high school reunion in 1998, I resisted the temptation to ask to see his worry mole again.

DR. PETRIE

Dr. Petrie who wrote *The Auburn Creed* was a beloved professor at Auburn for many years and was even the football coach there for a time. Once, my brother, seven years my senior, took me with him to Dr. Petrie's class. Leon had realized that Dr. Petrie would be a legend and thought I would like to say someday that I had had the experience of attending his class. He was right, and while I don't remember anything about that class, I do remember two stories that have come down through the years.

In those days of the late 1930's, hazing of freshmen as I have noted was alive and well on the Auburn campus. In the freshman class, there was a student who strongly physically resembled Dr. Petrie, except Dr. Petrie was slick bald with just a fringe of hair extending about one finger's breadth above his ears downward only. A shave of this student's head, except as noted above, made him a young look-alike. He was sent in late to Dr. Petrie's class, for maximum effect, just as Dr. Petrie started his lecture.

Dr. Petrie noticed the joke immediately and in going along with it said, "Dr. Petrie, you are late this morning. Please come and take charge of your class."

The quick thinking freshman stepped to the lectern and said, "Thank you. For tomorrow, review the next chapter. Class dismissed."

On another, much earlier occasion, Dr. Petrie in administering an exam noticed one of the students apparently making use of some notes under the large French cuffs that were in vogue in those days. Dr. Petrie approached the student addressing him, "Young man, may I see underneath your cuff?" The student had stood as was the respectful response back then and said, "Yes, Sir."

Turning the cuff back, Dr. Petrie found, printed on the student's wrist, "You are a fool for looking!" Dr. Petrie was said to have enjoyed the joke.

A part of Dr. Petrie's legacy lives on in *The Auburn Creed*, which he wrote.

THE AUBURN CREED
I believe that this is a practical world and that I can count only on what I earn. Therefore, I believe in work . . . hard work.

I believe in education, which gives me the knowledge to work wisely and trains my mind and my hands to work skillfully.

I believe in honesty and truthfulness, without which I cannot win the respect and confidence of my fellow men.

I believe in a sound mind in a sound body and a spirit that is not afraid, and in clean sports that develop these qualities.

l believe in obedience to law because it protects the rights of all.

I believe in the human touch, which cultivates sympathy with my fellow men and mutual helpfulness and brings happiness for all.

I believe in my country because it is a land of freedom and because it is my own home, and that I can best serve that country by "doing justly, loving mercy, and walking humbly with my God."

And because Auburn men and women believe in these things, I believe in Auburn and love it.

– Dr. George Petrie

OJT (On the Job Training)

Mr. John C. Ball Sr., local Auburn character, now long dead, was often seen on Toomer's Corner joshing and teasing his friends and strangers alike. One day as he held forth with his arms draped over the postal service letter drop box, a local policeman asked him, "What are you doing, Mr. Ball?"

Ever the jokester, he replied, "I'm doing on the job training."

"On the job training for what?"

Mr. Ball replied, "To be an Auburn policeman!"

HONEST MONEY

In my youth we called adult – especially elderly – black persons *aunt* or *uncle* as a title of respect. We have, of course, the *Uncle Remus Stories* by Joel Chandler Harris, Aunt Jemima pancake mix, and Uncle Ben's rice as holdovers from this era.

During WW II years almost everything was in short supply and many staple goods were rationed. There were some who stocked up on the more limited items, but all in all, our country was extremely united.

With this background, as the story goes, an elderly black lady entered the Bank of Auburn, in those days located on the NW corner of N. College and W. Magnolia, carrying in her hand a brown paper poke [bag]. Clark Hudson greeted her and asked what he might do for her. She allowed as how she'd like to open a bank account.

Standing behind the teller's window, he received the poke and dumped the contents onto the work area. There were several ten dollar bills, an occasional twenty dollar bill, still more five dollar bills, and quite a few crumpled, even folded one dollar bills. Somewhat taken aback at this lady's having a considerable amount of money for that time, he said innocently, "My, my Auntie, you've been hoarding."

Drawing herself to her full five feet three or four inches, she said pointedly, "No suh, ah hain't – this here's honest money!"

FAVORITE UNCLES

LAWRENCE

My two favorite uncles were Lawrence Cox and Joe Wright. Lawrence was my mother's only brother and Joe was my mother's brother-in-law. I don't know why, but in our family, for the most part, uncles and aunts were called by their given names without titles. This seemed to me to make our bond closer.

Lawrence's son Ray, two years my junior, and I gained our initial experience smoking by scarfing Lawrence's cigar butts and re-lighting them. We never O.D.'d because he smoked them

Cousins Ray Cox and Joseph Wright; Arab, Alabama, circa 1947

so short that there wasn't enough left except for a puff or two each. When Ray was a little guy and picking up on naughty words, Lawrence would spell these words. As a consequence the family word for "ass" was "double a jess r" which was Ray's verbal attempt to break the code.

Lawrence was a fun uncle, not just because of his sense of humor, which was remarkable, but also because of his somewhat adventuresome spirit. He bought a new 1936 Ford that had a radio, the first in-car radio that I had ever seen.

Once when returning to Alabama from South Carolina, he missed the desired highway in downtown Atlanta, and the ladies on the trip became quite upset at being lost in the big city in the middle of the night. He calmly replied, "I like to get lost once in a while – it causes me to think." He loved football almost to the exclusion of all other sports and expressed his fondness by saying, "I'd rather hear the whistle for the opening kickoff of just any high school football game than see the whole World Series in person." (Radio and in person were the only ways to experience sports events in those days.) Lawrence's other son, Gene, maintains the family love of football and is a veritable encyclopedia of football knowledge, in general, and of Auburn football, in particular.

My favorite remembrance of Lawrence involved a squirrel hunt. As Lawrence, Ray, and I skirted the hardwood trees, he led the way with me following a few steps behind. As we were entering the area to be hunted, the .22 caliber rifle I was carrying, which had but recently been given Lawrence by my brother Ralph, fired with the bullet's striking the ground near his foot as we walked along. He turned toward me with blanched face exclaiming, but without anger, "What in the world happened?"

I, as shaken as he, replied, "I don't know, Lawrence, but I had my hand nowhere near the trigger."

He asked me to show how and where I was holding the rifle. He then ejected the fired cartridge, chambered a fresh round, and then pointing the rifle in a safe direction, had me place his hand exactly as mine had been. We waited, and waited, and waited. After what seemed a long time, but probably was only three or four minutes, the rifle again fired.

Lawrence simply said, "We'll take this rifle to the house and never take it out again."

Lawrence Cox family: Ray, Gene, Cora Lee, and Lawrence; Arab, Alabama. Photo circa Mid-1940s

I have relived this frightening experience again and again. I am so thankful that the defective rifle fired again, un-indicting me. Most of all, I was thankful that my uncle was uninjured, and that he was an understanding uncle who did not lash out at me, barely a teenager, with an accusation of careless and irresponsible behavior. Lawrence was rotund and short of stature, physically, but he stood tall as a southern pine in my eyes that day. Now, nearly sixty years after this incident, he is still "tall in the saddle" in my memory.

In 1961 he experienced a stroke that affected his ability to swallow, leading to his having great difficulty in handling his saliva. He would no longer eat with the family because of this, and on the rare occasions when he went out, he carried a small kidney basin containing a few tissues in order to have a place to expectorate. Once when he went to town and was moving slowly down Main Street and holding on to his basin, someone in his/her compassion put in a quarter. However well intentioned, this hurt his pride and assaulted his independence.

As a youngster, I gained the impression that he was my richest relative. This was based on a simple observation, in that he bought oranges by the sack, placed them on the back porch, and we could have one anytime we wished without asking.

He enriched my childhood, was one of my two favorite uncles, and I treasure my memory of him.

JOE

Joe Wright, my other favorite uncle, was the hardest working man I ever knew. A farmer, he arose at 4:30 a.m. year-round. Living in a home without electricity or running water, he had a lot of chores to do including caring for the mules and hogs, milking the cow, cutting and splitting firewood, as the house was heated by a fireplace and cooking was done on a wood stove. Getting to bed on a winter night was a carefully orchestrated routine. First, one rotisseried himself in front of the open fire, then made a mad dash to the turned-down bed. Using as

Joe and Ida Belle Wright; Arab, Alabama, 1940s

few steps on the cold linoleum-covered floor as possible, we dived into the featherbed. Sleeping in a featherbed is, itself, a unique experience; the feather-filled quilt, after acclimating to body temperature, envelops one with a warm embrace that has a comforting clasp that is hard to describe, but once warmed, one feels not only warm, but secure.

As I grew up and before completing high school, I would often spend several days in the summer visiting and sometimes helping Joe on the farm. One experience, now a page out of the past, was trading with the peddler who took chickens, eggs, and other items in trade for candy treats and necessities. The sight of his rickety truck with chicken coops sometimes suspended from the sides as he came down the farm road was a welcomed diversion.

My sojourns on the farm were marked with losses as well as gains. I lost my college ring one summer and was never able to find it, but that loss pales in the wonderful light of the fond memories I experienced there.

Joe's treasured possession was a Parker double barrel shotgun. Brought out on certain occasions to be seen anew and admired, it was a Parker Trojan, the cheapest grade, but I thought it quite grand. Joe's son, Joseph, along with Ray, Lawrence's son, were the two cousins with whom I had the closest association when my growing-up years were filled with our adventures on my summer visits to Arab.

In May 1960, when I was a junior in medical school, my father had a fatal stroke. After the funeral, as I was saying goodbye to Joe and his wife, my aunt Ida Belle, he said, "Wait a minute, I want to give you something." When he came out of the house, he brought the shotgun saying to me, "I want you to have this. I have a feeling I won't ever see you again." I protested, but he was quite adamant, so, thanking him, I took the gun. He was right, as he died in the fall of that year.

The shotgun, a reminder of a wonderful uncle and grand times spent with family, lived with me for thirty-nine years – until three years ago when I gave the gun to Joseph who will treasure it and pass it on to one of his two sons.

Glenn with Nell Shelton Jones and Hazel Shelton Boyd, Arab neighbors, who were my babysitters in the early 1930s. They found that a tomato stem complete with "petals" placed on the porch near the steps was enough of a spider look-alike to keep me away from the steps. Photo taken in Arab, Alabama, 2000.

UNDERGRADUATE PHARMACY SCHOOL

In September 1947, I enrolled, in the school of pharmacy at A.P. I. (Alabama Polytechnic Institute, Auburn University as of 1960, and hereafter referred to as Auburn University or just simply Auburn, as used by the locals). That was quite an experience as the WW II veterans were everywhere. With their background and experience, they provided formidable competition in the academic arena. In those days, the pharmacy school shared office and some lecture and laboratory space with the school of chemistry in Ross Chemistry building while most of the pharmacy lectures and labs were held in a WW II wood temporary building which was cold in the winter and hot, very hot in the summer. We had classes starting as early as 7:00 a.m. with the last class beginning as late as 5:00 p. m. which, if one had both, made for a very long day.

PROFESSOR GEORGE A. HARGREAVES

Professor George A. Hargreaves was my favorite professor and was the hands-down favorite of most of the other students as well. He was cheerful, approachable, and knowledgeable about what was going on around campus, especially the pharmacy school. His exams were fair and thorough, perhaps accounting for his popularity among the students. In addition to his teaching duties in the school of pharmacy, he was the A.P.I./Auburn golf coach.

Calling on him in 1950 for a recommendation for graduate school in pharmacy at Purdue University, I discovered that he was pleased to have been asked and was very complimentary of me in his letter; however, the Korean War canceled my plans for Purdue graduate school.

One day in an expression of his humor, Professor Hargreaves stated, "LSMFT (Lucky Strike Means Fine Tobacco, long the sales pitch for that brand of cigarettes) was really LSFMT, Lord Save us From Mr. Truman," a commentary on the draft for the Korean War.

DEAN L. S. BLAKE

This favorite professor served under Dean Blake, a rather benign fellow who had a right smart bark but not much bite. However, I never had any trouble with him.

One day as Dean Blake was on his way to class to give an exam, he stopped to talk with Professor Hargreaves who looked at a copy of the exam and said, "Dean Blake, this is the same exam you gave last quarter. The dean replied, "I know it – I just changed the damn answers."

In addition to Professor Hargreaves, and Dean Blake, the two remaining characters from pharmacy school whose names stir memories of the pleasant, the unpleasant, and the humorous are Professor P^2 and Professor Nickel.

PROFESSOR A. F. NICKEL

Professor A. F. Nickel was a tough taskmaster and brooked no levity with students. On the first day in Operative Pharmacy I (his first class with the freshmen), he directed everyone to, "Look at the student on your left, now look at the student on your right, now think about yourself." He then said, "Historically, one of the three of you will not complete this course, at least on the first try." This prediction came true. He paced the laboratory somewhat like a caged tiger, sometimes abruptly challenging the student when pacing the floor, and if he stopped behind you, LOOK OUT!

The day he stopped behind me, with every eye in the laboratory on me, he said, "Marsh, what are you making?" I replied, "Senna infusion, Sir."

"And how are you to filter it?" he asked.

"With a pledget of cotton, Sir," I replied. He plunged his hand and wrist into the large funnel reservoir whence the infusion was being filtered, withdrew the displeasing – to him – amount of cotton, and held it up for all to see, squeezed it so that the fluid gushed out of the cotton, and thus, spattered all over my shoes. His comment: "My God, your old man must be a cotton farmer and you are trying to raise the price of cotton." With that, he threw the soggy cotton ball to the floor with all the force he could muster, and yelled, "MAKE IT AGAIN."

"Yes, Sir," I said lamely.

In this same class, we had a student, R. T. B., whose nickname was Hezzy. Think of the most country character ever on the *Andy Griffith* TV show and you have the picture. Professor Nickel usually started his class by asking a student a question, and on this day, he directed the question to R. T. B. To everyone's great surprise, Hezzy replied with the correct answer. This also surprised Professor Nickel and in his clipped way of speaking, he demanded, "Blake, did you know that or did you guess?"

"Waaaal, Fessor, ah reckon hit wuz a leetle bit o' both." Resounding laughter and applause ensued. R. T. B. also had the last laugh – he became the V.P. of a giant pharmaceutical firm.

Professor P ^{2}

The last in this group of illustrative Auburn professors, I need not identify by name. This long time professor of Chemistry is best known by the appellation P ^{2} (his initials). He taught quantitative analysis which was a required course for all pharmacy majors. In this course, we soon learned that he was most irritated by members of the class inappropriately weighing re-agents on the analytical balances, first, by the weighing of too large amounts on the most sensitive and precise balances and secondly, trying to weigh very small amounts on scales which should have been used for large amounts.

This perplexed him to no end, especially when questioning the students as to the rationale for such laboratory procedure. The all-too-familiar response by the students when so ques-tioned was the nonspecific excuse, "They told me to."

Having heard more than he wished of this excuse, he ex-ploded during the next lecture recounting his, "They told me to" experiences to the class. In no uncertain terms, he then thun-dered, "Students (pronounced stoo-dints), I have been to the registrar's office at this university and there is no 'Mr. They' reg-istered in any class 'nowheres' at this university!"

That was the very last we heard of "They told me to."

Speaking of being a pharmacy major, Professor P² had a decided distaste for pharmacy students and was not hesitant to deride students identified thereby on registrar printout by the symbol PY. His general assessment was that pharmacy students could not think and instead substituted memorization. Indeed, one of his favorite statements was, "The difference between people and monkeys is that monkeys can think." No one had ever heard of a pharmacy student's making an A in one of his classes until one of my colleagues went to him and acknowl-edged that the Professor's allegations against pharmacy students were true and that he (the student) had been enlightened and was changing his major to Pre-Med. The ruse worked – that pharmacy student received an A, but graduated with a degree in Pharmacy.

Professor P² had some strange opinions, as the reader is becoming aware. In class one day, he opined that students com-ing to Auburn enrolled often in engineering and could not make the grade. They would then change their major to chemistry and again, could not pass. After a succession of academic failures, according to Professor P[2], the student would then finally change to the School of Education where he/she would succeed. As the climax to this story, he would thunder, "We have the dummies teaching our children!" Many times during his lectures, he would pause and repeat, "Thinking (pronounced THEENKing) is a painful process."

I didn't get an A in this course, but considered my B the equivalent. I was sort of intrigued by this character and took geology under him as an elective in 1949 or 1950.

He had a kind of sing-song way of lecturing, never made out a class roll but instead, kept the registrar's sheets in his book which being larger than the book, curled badly and became quite dog-eared. However, this untidiness did not extend to the blackboard. He insisted upon its being impeccable, and before class began would erase it over and over and even moisten the tip of his finger with saliva and apply this to a resistant fleck of chalk on the board. Sometimes for the most resistant chalk spots, he would scrape with his fingernail. When the blackboard passed inspection, he would then place all of the chalk, bits and pieces, and new unused pieces alike at one end of the chalk/eraser tray under the blackboard and the erasers were similarly herded to the other end. When this fetish was completed, he was finally ready to teach. I never did see the man smile, but he did a substitute action by showing his teeth, keeping his teeth clamped together and causing the perioral muscles to contract, exposing his teeth fully.

After the first geology exam had been graded, the roll taken, and the exam papers passed out to the class, he looked out over the class and after the requisite substitute smile, said, "Those papers were like Texas papers – full of wide open spaces." Another substitute smile and he further noted, "Those papers were like Texas papers for another reason too – two wide points with a lot of bull in between," followed by yet another substitute smile.

Once when he was teaching his chemistry class which he pronounced "Cheemistree," a farmer brought into the dean's office an object that he had plowed up in his field. Thinking it to be a huge diamond, he would not wait for the chemistry class to be over, but proceeded to the lecture room and knocked on the door. He handed the object to Professor P² who carefully examined it, and as part of his assessment, took it to the window, "winder" as it is pronounced in Alabama, to see

Glenn, freshman, Alabama Polytechnic Institute (now Auburn University), 1948

if it were hard enough to etch the glass. It was not. Professor P² studied it again, handed it back to the farmer, remarking that it looked like "quartz" to him.

The farmer asked, "Quarts of what?" which broke up the class.

In those long-ago days, student privacy was not an issue, so the grades were posted opposite the students' names in the window of the professor's office. As I was looking for my grade in geology, Professor P² happened to come out of his office and said, "Well, Marsh, you were close to an A – but not close enough." He rewarded me then with his substitute smile as I left his presence with my B+. Good as it gets for a pharmacy major.

I graduated from pharmacy school having been elected to membership in Rho Chi, the national honor society for pharmacy students.

ARMY SERVICE

Korean War

The Korean War, which had broken out in 1950, the same year I graduated from pharmacy school, changed everything for me. Drafted in December, I reported to Fort Chaffee, Arkansas for infantry basic training.

First of all, I didn't think much of Arkansas. Like most former service men whether Army, Navy, or Air Force, I did not like the state in which I had basic training. I will have to acknowledge, however, that the state had beautiful sunrises and sunsets since I saw one of each, up close everyday that I was there.

I was assigned to Company A, 81st Medium Tank Battalion, a troubled outfit, if there ever was one. Some of the problems included the company commander, who was relieved of command mid-training cycle because of alcoholism (scuttlebutt said). Food was being stolen from the mess hall to the degree we were on short rations. I saw fights and near fights over a slice of bread. Two of the cadre who were stealing our clothing were caught and punished. Our platoon sergeant, actually a corporal, with misplaced logic, felt that if our troops in Korea were cold that winter, we could empathize with them if we were cold too, so on his initiative alone, we were deprived of barracks' heat. Another of the cadre was drunk and decided that we should march in the rain on a December Sunday afternoon in our Class A uniforms, the dress uniform, not the usual fatigues. And so we did. Chaplain John D. Quick heard about it, and that episode was not repeated.

When we arrived at Fort Chaffee, the barracks had been closed since WW II, so we were assigned the formidable task of cleaning them, thus we got off to a bad start that continued. One of the few bright spots was the fact that my cousin Kirby Hays was in the same company, but not the same platoon, so I could go to his warm barracks next door to write letters. He had been working as an entomologist in Puerto Rico when he was drafted, but the Army needed riflemen and he, remaining in the infantry, was wounded in Korea, but we will come back to that.

Training ceased for Christmas Day only, so Kirby and I went over to the service club, a building for off-duty social functions for enlisted men. As we walked in, a recording of Bing Crosby singing, "I'll be Home for Christmas" was playing. We simultaneously stopped, turned facing each other, exchanged looks, and without a word, returned to our barracks, changed into our fatigues, and spent the day, writing letters. We were lonely and dejected, and if the truth be known, homesick.

I liked going to the rifle range although it was a several mile march. I really liked shooting and scored expert in this activity. One day as we were cleaning our rifles, I noticed one of the fellows in my platoon had gotten the cleaning patch and jag stuck in his rifle barrel, creating a barrel obstruction. Several people tugged and pounded, but the obstruction was not cleared. When we went to the rifle range the next day, I noticed that when this fellow's turn came to fire, his buddy furnished the rifle with which he had just completed firing. It so happened that when our platoon leader, an ROTC 2nd Lieutenant from Texas A & M, decided to fire the course, he unwittingly chose the bore-obstructed rifle from the rack and with ammunition in hand was proceeding to the firing line. I stopped him saying, "Sir, if I were you, I would not fire that weapon."

"Why?"

"It has a bore obstruction."

He lifted the rifle to look through the bore, could not, and with a marked pallor of his face said, "Thank you!" Had he fired this rifle, the cartridge case would have ruptured, as would have the barrel. Most likely, results would have been brass fragments in the face and eyes, with injuries also to the left hand and arm. There could also have been injuries to nearby persons.

Back to Kirby. While in Korea, his infantry outfit was assigned the task of taking a certain hill and during the action, he and his buddy dived into a shell crater during the advance. The firing died down and absolute silence ensued. While waiting for what seemed a long time, his buddy whispered, "I can't stand it. I've got to see what's going on." With that, he ever so slowly raised his head to peer over the edge of the hole. There was a solitary shot, and the buddy's lifeless body fell backward into Kirby's arms. Kirby then emptied both their rifles, while exposing as little of himself as possible, jumped out of their haven, and ran back to what had been his forward line. He was hit in the hand during his charge to the rear. Years later, I asked him what happened after that. He said, "I woke up in the psychiatry ward of the hospital."

"Why?"

"They said I was trying to dig a foxhole."

"What's wrong with that?"

"They didn't want one in the floor of the hospital."

Kirby recovered completely, earned a Ph.D. in entomology, and in time, became chairman of that department at Auburn University, prior to his untimely death from cancer. His widow and two daughters survive him. Interestingly, his brother Sidney retired a few years ago as chairman of the Entomology Department at Clemson University.

HERIOUS COTTON

Other than my cousin Kirby Hays, the only person whom I remembered from Infantry Basic Training at Fort Chaffee, Arkansas was my black friend Herious Cotton from Mississippi. Sitting beside him in chapel, I first noticed his marvelous bass voice. We had a good deal in common, and the racial difference bothered us not at all. Sadly, when I located and called him in the spring of 2001, I learned he had died but three months before my call. I felt very badly about this but did have a nice phone visit with his son and widow.

After finishing infantry basic training, I reported to Brooke Army Medical Center, San Antonio, Texas for medical basic training. Enroute there, I stopped at Waco, Texas to visit a friend from Auburn college days, Joe Patterson, who had transferred to Baylor University. The next day, along with a married couple, Joe and I were enroute to their respective churches where they were student pastors. Having rained the night before, it was a beautiful Sunday morning. East central Texas is especially nice in springtime with the blue bonnets and Indian paintbrush adding spice to life. As we drove along, we sang hymns and all was right with the world.

Suddenly, having a blowout, we coasted to the side of the road. Opening the trunk revealed a spare tire, lug wrench, but no jack. I spotted a farmhouse about a half-mile down the road and volunteered to scout up a jack.

Arriving at the house, I knocked on the door and was greeted by a large, heavyset man. Attired in a suit, he had a Bible and Sunday school quarterly clamped very tightly between his upper arm and chest. I immediately sized him up as a Baptist and most likely a Baptist deacon (it takes one to know one). I told him of our predicament, including the fact of two student preachers with congregations expecting them, and he responded to my request to borrow a jack saying, "I'd *shore* like to *hep* you boys, but I'm on my way to church and I'm already late."

I no longer remember how we managed to mount the spare; however, we did make it to worship on time. This remains one of my favorite stories of one's losing sight of the big picture.

During my training at Brooke, I met some wonderful fellows, optometrists such as James F. Cogan of Saratoga Springs, New York and pharmacists such as Noel Nuessle from Jennings, a suburb of St. Louis, and Don Pipkin of Bakersfield, California. I was later to be befriended by Noel's parents and spent many a weekend with them while stationed at the St. Louis Medical Depot. Jim Cogan and I renewed our friendship as he was already at the depot when I received orders to report there. We referred to ourselves as Willie and Joe of Bill Mauldin's WW II comic strip. I was Willie.

RHIP – Rank Has its Privileges

After my basic infantry training, Medical Field Service School training, and leadership school, I was assigned to a holding company, awaiting orders and perhaps, a direct commission as a Second Lieutenant in the Medical Service Corps.

I had several friends sharing this uncertainty and every few days, orders would arrive, and I'd have one less friend present. One of my closest friends received his orders and was to be commissioned the following day. We went out to dinner to celebrate this big event and had a very nice evening.

About mid-morning the next day, he came back to our barracks wearing his new uniform with spit shined shoes, gold, actually brass Second Lieutenant bars shining brightly and pants creased so sharply they would almost slice bread. As we stood there, his bags and baggage on the barracks floor, we all shook hands, wishing him well, bidding farewell, when he said to me, "Marsh, take my bags to my car."

I know my face must have mirrored my unbelieving ears, this, my friend of the evening before, now an officer, asserting his rank, telling me to be his servant. I didn't move. He spoke again saying, "That's an order."

I said to him, "Your bags will rot before I take them to your car," as I walked away to my bunk. He had plenty of witnesses if he had wished to charge me with insubordination, but I doubted if the other equally-shocked friends would have testified.

The lesson that I learned (again) is that friends are not always the friends they first seem to be.

My commission finally came through in August 1951. I then reported to the St. Louis Medical Depot as a brand new Second Lieutenant for training as a medical supply officer.

I spent six months there, and because of the proximity of the city library and my interest in history, I became a sort of expert on the subject of the James boys, Jesse and Frank. I also met the girl I was later to marry, Elisabeth Ann Stadnick. She was a secretary at the Depot and had grown up in St. Louis. After completing the medical supply course, I was assigned to Medical Field Service School in San Antonio, then to the medical section of the Atlanta General Depot, arriving there in 1952. I was the vault officer, responsible for vast stores of grain alcohol, dental gold and silver, and narcotics along with other duties. I enjoyed my year in Atlanta, and being close (118 miles) to Auburn, I was able to visit my parents frequently.

"Great Speckled Bird"

This story came to me, at the Depot, from a fellow officer, a veteran of WW II, who was called back into service for the Korean conflict and who witnessed the episode. As he described it, when WW II ended, the soldiers who were sent home first were the ones with the most dependents. In my friend's outfit there was a lonely mountaineer from Tennessee, who had somehow brought with him from the states a wind-up record player and but one record, Roy Acuff's version of "The Great Speckled Bird." In that tent, the first thing every morning and the last thing every night was this mournful dirge being played. The owner of the player and record was, on the basis of the number of his children, one of the very first to go home. On the morning of his departure, in an emotional, teary scene, he presented his player to the fellow in the next bunk, making much of how this player and record had been the source of great strength and determination that had seen him through the trials and tribulations of being away from his family. He then handed his buddy the record, who in one fluid motion gripped the record, one hand on each side, and broke it over his knee while concomitantly saying an insincere, "Thanks!"

INSPECTION

When I was a relatively new Second Lieutenant at the Depot, now Fort Willem, I was scheduled to inspect a training company on a Saturday morning, the traditional day and time for Army inspections.

I showed up as the inspecting officer, impeccable in my freshly pressed uniform, fresh haircut, and highly polished shoes, except for one item. I had forgotten to wear a tie. An observant Sergeant whispered this observation to me, and I decided on that basis to inspect the company supply section first. There, I was given my choice of dozens of regulation neckties – all were the same – and upon tying this item in the approved Army style, finished conducting my inspection. I don't remember the overall rating that I awarded, but you may be sure that the company supply received an outstanding rating.

In general, the military is a non-thinking man's world – or was in those days – consisting of a rule and often a sign covering every situation. I remember one such sign in an Army facility in Atlanta *inside* an elevator that boldly stated, "Open elevator door before exiting elevator."

How else?

However, the Army had a few statements worthy of remembering, one of which was, "Be at the proper place, in the proper uniform (dress), at the proper time, in the proper condition for duty." I'd like to see this adhered to in this twenty-first century with universal day-to-day application.

UFO's

Those days in the fifties were UFO days, and "sightings" were rampant. There were stories of people's being abducted by alien space ships and then these people would be set free and interviewed with results in the tabloids. The more things change, the more they stay the same.

As luck would have it, someone phoned in a UFO report when I was officer of the day at the Atlanta General Depot, so it was my duty to check it out. Driving to the area where it was reportedly seen, I took a fifteen-minute nap, and upon my return reported, "No UFO seen." Yes, I did see one "Marshian" – in the rear view mirror.

SPEECHLESS

Being a strongly family-oriented fellow back then in the early nineteen fifties (still am), when 4:30 p. m. Friday came, unless I had weekend duty, I was anxiously making my way to Auburn, Alabama to spend the weekend with my mother and father.

When in haste one Friday, trying to beat rush hour, I was speeding. A military police car pulled me over just as I exited the gate leaving the depot. A few more feet and I'd have been off government property and home free. As the MP came walking toward my window, I remembered some cookies I had on the front seat. He began his spiel about my speeding, and I sensed that he was not a seasoned, experienced MP, and before he opened his citation book, I thrust several cookies upon him, insisting that he have one, now another, right then, and when he did so, nearly unable to talk with his mouth full of cookies, I thanked him in nonstop words, and drove off seeing him in the rear view mirror, as he fumbled for his whistle with crumbs falling out of his mouth.

No matter, he couldn't have blown it. No way!

In late winter 1953, I was ordered to US Army Forces Far East. I had bought my first car, a used 1951 Ford, the year before, and as I headed west for port of embarkation, I stopped to visit Leon in Abilene, Texas. Continuing on the way, I bought a personal sidearm in Lubbock, Texas, from where I drove to San Diego, visited Knotts Berry Farm, Serven Gun Room, and looked up my friend Don Pipkin, who was now in the Navy as the pharmacy officer on the hospital ship *USS Repose*.

That is a story in itself as Don and I were together in leadership school, then the holding company. With his Army commission coming before mine, he was then ordered to Indiantown Gap, Pennsylvania, and while there, his Navy commission came through. At this late date, I no longer remember how, but he was able to get out of the Army and into the Navy which he much preferred. We celebrated St. Patrick's Day 1953, with a nice visit on his ship and dinner ashore.

When I proceeded to Oakland, I learned there was a glut of cars on the west coast, with values depressed, so Don's parents graciously agreed to keep my car until my return. After the usual delays, we boarded the troop ship, *USNS Gen. M. C. Meigs*, for Japan. The first night, there were quite a few who became seasick. Interestingly, coming up from below deck the next morning, we were astounded to find that we were still tied up at dockside. This event has something to say about mind over matter. Finally underway, we sailed past Alcatraz and under the Golden Gate Bridge. We were on our way – but we weren't. The troop ship turned around and returning under the bridge, we stopped. Someone started a rumor that the Korean War was over, and that we weren't needed. That, however, was just wishful thinking, so after a few minutes, we were underway for real.

The most memorable events of this voyage were experiencing an Easter sunrise worship service at sea and making friends with a chaplain and a young pharmacist, a graduate of the University of Tennessee. In about ten days or so we reached Yokohama, Japan and debarked to the strains of "Pretend You're Happy When You're Blue," sung by Nat "King" Cole.

I was immediately impressed with the Japanese people whom I encountered. They were very neat, clean, orderly, honest, thrifty, energetic, and polite. After several days, we embarked for Pusan, Korea, and interestingly, we smelled Korea about the time that we came into view of that country. It had an odor something akin to an improperly functioning waste disposal or sewer. From Pusan, we traveled for assignment to Seoul, Korea where 8th Army Headquarters was located. The journey by train was less than pleasant. All passengers were military, crowded into the available space with limited sanitary facilities that consisted of a good-sized hole in the floor of the train at the end of the car where one could void with no privacy whatsoever. As this trip took place on a Sunday, I asked the senior officer in the car for permission to hold worship services. Permission was granted, and as I always carried a copy of the *New Testament*, I conducted the services. As the railroad car was already full of personnel, only those in that particular car were able to participate.

I wasn't very impressed with the paper shufflers at 8th Army and not at all with the officer in charge of assigning medical personnel. He was exactly like the character played by Robert Duvall in the movie *Apocalypse Now*, made many years later. His hair was closely cropped, maybe even shaved, and he wore a scarf, consisting of a torn remnant of camouflage parachute material. He was a bundle of forced energy and appeared as a caricature of General George Patton. I was distinctly uncomfortable around this man. Stories about him abounded. For example, he'd gotten a medal for driving a loaded army truck out of a burning building, and on another occasion, after a staff meeting, instead of exiting the room by the doorway, he leaped out of the window, informing the others, "I'm airborne, you know." I thought him mostly hoax, but with his rank, position, and peculiar personality, a cause for concern. This proved to be true much later that year because as peace negotiations were going on and after a truce was signed, medical personnel were among the last – in fact – on the last troop ship home before Christmas. Combat personnel on the line, i.e. infantry, artillery, had been long gone before we boarded the ship for home.

WESTERN MOVIE FAN

I had been in Korea less than a week when I was standing on the side of a muddy road thumbing a ride. All military vehicles traditionally stopped for any G.I. attempting to catch a ride. As I stood there waiting for a military vehicle to come along, a young Korean lad of ten or twelve years of age walked up, stood in front of me, looked me up and down, walked all the way around me, came back, and stood precisely in front of me, bowed quite formally and said, "Number one cowboy pistol."

In Korea the very best was number one while number ten was the worst. Apparently, he had seen enough American movies, westerns, of course, to appreciate my Colt revolver and holster.

The First Medical Field Laboratory, the unit to which I was assigned, was located on the compound of the 121st Evacuation Hospital at Yong-Dong-Po, a village across the Han River, south of Seoul, Korea, where I was detachment commander, motor officer, and supply officer, in addition to having other duties.

In Korea there were some situations that required getting used to. Korea was the type of place where one had to think positive thoughts, as there were so many opportunities to encounter the unpleasant. As a reminder, I had someone paint a sign, "I cried because I had no shoes until I met the man who had no feet." I did not wish to forget my good fortune.

TWO FOR ONE

When I arrived in Korea, I quickly noticed that all the pencils had been sawn in half – one-half, of course, having no eraser, but since the Army didn't make mistakes, they weren't really

Glenn writing a letter while awaiting assignment, shortly after arriving in Korea. The "Number One Cowboy pistol" is shown to advantage. Yong Dong Po, Korea, June 1953

needed. I failed to see the logic in this attempt to alleviate the shortage of pencils as two or three sharpenings, at most, caused each half of the pencil to be too short to be used, so they were thrown away and a new one-half pencil put into service which resulted in each whole pencil lasting through only half-dozen sharpenings in the Army M-1 modification.

Thus, rather than alleviating the shortage, it was exacerbated.

Work was seven days a week, but Sundays were different. We received our weekly malaria medication as we went through the chow line, and the chapel was open if one cared to attend. Food was wholesome, plentiful, well prepared, and except for one or two things, similar to stateside. Eggs were different, however. They were cold storage.

Fresh, they were not. When the shell was broken and the contents were placed on the griddle, there were not the two or even sometimes three tiers of a fresh egg – just one, and it spread over the cooking surface like water, requiring the attention of two cooks. Thus, as one cook cracked the egg, released it onto the griddle, the other cook quickly did his best to hem it up, or it would spread out the size of a large plate. The flavor was accentuated with a rather strong character like a year-old pecan or walnut as compared to a fresh nut. I became used to this flavor and upon my return to the states, found a fresh egg somewhat tasteless. I hasten to add, once home, I have for decades been used to fresh eggs and no longer would wish one from cold storage.

The largest gastronomic hurdle to overcome was the lack of fresh veggies, especially lettuce, tomatoes, cucumbers, and carrots. On occasion, and quite uncommonly, we'd have raw cabbage, but never any of the above.

Papasan and the Tomato

One day, however, Papasan, Yu Chi Kun, brought me a lovely fresh, red, ripe tomato. This was a really big deal with food of any sort being so scarce to him and his family. I thanked him profusely, and during the day looked at it several times picking it up and closely examining it. I longed for that tomato. I imagined its taste. However, knowing that *night soil*, human excrement, was used as fertilizer, I did not consume the tomato. I no longer remember what I told him upon seeing him the day after receiving the gift.

Man of the House

Yu Chi Kun whom we irritated by calling "You chew gum" always responded by saying, "My name not *You Chew Gum*; my name Yu Chi Kun," and then he'd laugh, as he knew we were laughing with him, not at him. He did odd jobs about the laboratory, and we'd sneak him food from the mess hall. I went by

Papasan, Yu Chi Kun, Korean citizen. Employee of 1ˢᵗ Medical Field Laboratory, Yong Dong Po, Korea 1953. Affectionately known to the soldiers as You Chew Gum.

his home once, inadvertently at mealtime, and he and his oldest son were eating while his wife and younger children were waiting to eat until the two males were finished. I asked him about this, and he let me know that he was "honcho" meaning "boss" and that was that. No further discussion welcome. He and I got along well, and I occasionally think of him, but he is, no doubt, now deceased.

We had armed forces radio and *Stars and Stripes*, the Korea edition newspaper, and at night the radio programming was made to coincide with popular shows back home. For instance, one would hear "Hit Parade" on Saturday nights. On one special Saturday night, later in the programming, when I was listening to the Grand Ole Opry, just as the vocalist finished, we heard a rousing "War Eagle" from the audience, no doubt by Auburn students who were in Nashville for the Auburn-Vanderbilt basketball game. What a thrill.

Shower day was a happening. We were allocated showers two to three times weekly. On shower day, we hiked with shaving kit, change of clean clothes, and towel in hand to the shower point. Water trailers were there as well as heaters for the water, and we then had our showers in portable units.

I found the chapel services on Sunday a.m. quite sterile, but Rev. A. B. Chestnut, a Church of God missionary, was a blessing, indeed, as he conducted services on Sunday night. Military personnel came from long distances in large numbers for these services, and the hospital commander was quite taken aback that the "official" services on Sunday a.m. were poorly attended. He directed that the hospital Chaplain attend on Sunday night and give him a personal report. As a result, taking an offering on Sunday night was prohibited. Others and I simply slipped our tithes into Rev. Chestnut's shirt pocket. We noted that the chaplain when needed could usually be found at the bar in the officer's club.

Irresponsible Behavior

One night in Korea when I was officer of the day, I saw a person lying in front of a jeep, actually half under the jeep against the left front wheel. He was a Lieutenant who had passed out, apparently while unsuccessfully trying to get into the driver's seat and had, in his drunken stupor, crawled to the position where found. I took him to the hospital, took possession of his sidearm, and left instructions with the personnel to send him to see me when he became sober.

He was one sheepish and cowed individual the next day. Greatly relieved to have his weapon returned, he thanked me profusely and I never saw him again.

Bedtime Snack

During air raid alarms in Korea, we would issue small arms to the troops, but no ammunition, and take our duty stations in total blackout. The searchlights played over the sky, and we'd listen for the sound of a single engine aircraft that we called

Glenn and his Jeep at Yong Dong Po, Korea, 1953

"Bed Check Charlie." He'd come about the time we'd be asleep in order to interrupt our sleep. Often we'd pass the time fantasizing about what we'd most like to eat stateside. My choice was always a hamburger and fries with a Coca-Cola.

VOICE FROM THE DEAD

There was a very funny story circulating around the hospital concerning one of our enlisted men who worked on one of the wards in the hospital. Incidentally, the hospital, 121st Evacuation Hospital, was housed in a burned out, gutted Korean building two or three stories tall. Because of its sturdy construction, it did not collapse during or after the fire. The original roof was almost totally gone, but the new one worked reasonably well. Through the ingenuity of some G.I., the attic flooring was repaired enough to support a shallow lake of melted tar which hardened, preventing most leaks. Surprisingly, it actually sufficed rather well.

Back to the subject at hand, as this humorous story goes, there was an enlisted man who was told, at night during his shift, that a body in the morgue had been sent there without the requisite identification tag affixed to the right big toe per regulation. He was handed the tag and a flashlight, as there was no electricity in the morgue. He made his way to the morgue, located at some little distance to isolate it from the hospital. With the light of the flashlight, he located the screen door that opened inwardly, entered, found the dark green plastic body bag, unzipped the full-length zipper down to foot level, slid his hand down the body's right leg to the foot, and isolated the toe. Just as he tied the knot securing the tag, the "body" said in a deep, sepulchral voice, "That's the wrong toe."

Having recently been to the morgue in daytime, I had noticed that the door now opened outwardly. The G.I. telling me the story had caused that modification.

He told me the story as I was on duty as officer of the day, checking the guards. Recognizing his name on the guard roster and wanting to hear the story firsthand, I had requested the blow-by-blow account of the event. Since the toe-tying episode, he had gotten into some trouble, so he was now permanently assigned to guard duty. Seemed to me a funny way to run a railroad, i.e. to take a guy who was not dependable enough to work on the train crew and yet assign him to guard the train. Only in the Army does this make sense.

On occasion, Army business would require a trip to Seoul where I found the black market thriving. On one occasion in a back alley stall, I found and purchased some books of poetry that have served me well. They were printed in the USA during the WW II years. I still enjoy them.

On more than one occasion, my trips to Seoul would take me past one of the saddest sights of all. This was the RTO, Rail Transportation Office, like our United States train depots. Sunday was the day that people came from far and near to that location to try to find friends and relatives, whom they had not seen since separation by war.

When fall came, and we were issued wool clothing, I was also able to supply my former high school classmate, John Lowery, army wool shirts and pants. He'd been forced to wear cotton uniforms while sitting in the cockpit of his plane "on ready" as the cold weather Air Force clothing had not arrived. John was an F-86 fighter pilot, located not too far from Yong Dong Po where I was able to visit him. John was also to meet Don Pipkin when we were able to go to Inchon where the *USS Repose* was anchored. All had a grand time. Sammie Lee, the Olympic diver, made a tour of military installations, and John, who was visiting me at the time, was pleased to meet him.

Being motor pool officer afforded me my own jeep and all the gasoline I needed. I also took a trip up to the front lines where I noticed the British had a teahouse. The consensus of most American troops that I talked to was that the Brits were indifferent combat soldiers. In contradistinction to the reputation that the British had for not being very willing fighters, the fiercest soldiers that I saw were Turks. I understood that they walked guard duty armed only with a knife, and in fact, went AWOL (absent without leave) from the hospital where they were patients, to make their way back to the front to fight.

There was a beautiful stateside type concrete bridge that US forces had built which I crossed, but I understand that in the truce agreement, we fell back a certain distance, leaving the bridge in the demilitarized zone, unused by anyone.

General Maxwell Taylor, 8th Army Commander, on an inspection trip, walked through our laboratory. I remember him as being of a very short stature.

KOREAN LANGUAGE

For all of the poverty and other problems evident in Korea, their language was far more precise than ours. For instance, they had separate words for *nephew* depending upon whether the nephew was from the bride's or the groom's side of the family. This also extended to aunts, uncles and these examples illustrate what I mean.

Their language achieved new highs (or lows) in that there was a word for "ladies of the evening" frequented by Americans, with a different name for those in the same profession frequented by the North Koreans.

A Life Wasted

The saddest event of my Korean tour happened on my tour of duty as officer of the day. We officers slept in a Quonset hut which can be envisioned as a giant corrugated steel drain pipe sliced lengthwise, the sliced side placed on a plank floor and the ends closed in, having a door on each end. There were no windows, but opaque, corrugated plastic four by eight (I guess) sheets spaced along the walls let in some light during the day. A stove, nearer one end than the other end, furnished heat, and leaving the door or doors open furnished cooling. We slept on cots with a frame over them to support the mosquito netting.

My cot, called a bunk, was nearest the back door on the left, farthest from the stove. As did practically all G.I.'s, I slept in my under shorts. Early one morning, as it was just getting daylight the CQ (Charge of Quarters) who stayed awake all night, observing for fire or other unusual events, awoke me with a repeated, "Come quick, something terrible has happened." That was all I could get from him. Over and over, he repeated this. I was awake immediately, threw back the mosquito net, jammed my feet into my boots without taking time to put on socks or tie my boots, strapped on my side arm, jammed my steel pot (helmet) on my head, and charged out the door in my underwear fully expecting to see thousands of North Korean or Chinese paratroopers coming down over the chopper landing strip and hospital compound. I followed the CQ with shoelaces flying, and helmet bouncing up and down on my head, but with the pistol still holstered.

There were no enemy soldiers, only total silence. I cannot forget the CQ's high pitched, nearly hysterical voice saying, "There, there," and there he was, the body of one of our medical officers, as army doctors are called, slumped up against the wire mesh screen behind which much of our laboratory supplies were stored. My run came to an abrupt halt. I did not recognize, from the rear, the partially clad, actually, almost fully clothed body, missing only shirt and cap. I touched the body, which was cold, with no pulse. I gently eased it forward, which was not easy as his feet were on the floor. It was Jim, my physician friend with whom I had eaten the prior evening meal, his last, and with whom I had walked to the shower point to get our showers, just a few hours before. I cut him down and noted how meticulously he had encircled, with adhesive tape, the long surgical gauze, a makeshift "rope," every few inches for added strength. I was astounded to note his bent knees. He could have, at one point in the tragedy, stood and been home free. He truly wanted to die. Of course, even with his slight frame, his weight, for even a few hours, would cause some stretching, both of the gauze and of the wire cage.

I summoned the proper people, recorded a list of witnesses at the scene by then, and went through his personal effects. At his bunk was the pocket book edition of Shakespeare's *King Lear*, the book turned upside down to mark his place. He was slightly more than half way through the play. He did not smoke, as best I remember, but had a new Zippo lighter engraved, "To Dr. Young, Best wishes, The boys." The boys were lab technicians of all ages. He had recently received orders to Japan, as he had completed his tour of duty in Korea. There was no coinage, as we used paper script in Korea, but there were some keys to fit, I don't know what, and his billfold. I counted the money, entered the amount on an inventory list, placed it and the billfold in an envelope and sealed it. I remember nothing else of his possessions, though, of course, he had uniforms and a kit with the usual shaving and dental care gear. I do remember reporting to the executive officer, as it was now the beginning of a new workday, and I was now the old officer of the day to be replaced by the new officer of the day within a matter of minutes.

That executive officer, I did not like. He was, essentially, without personality and was a stickler for dotting the *i*'s and crossing the *t*'s. When I reported Jim's death to this bean counter as Capt. James Young, he asked how I had recorded his death. I just knew he would ask that question and was ready with the answer, "Capt. James Young was coded for record only." I don't even remember what that phrase means, but it meant a lot to this officer who said, "Good!" He dismissed me. I saluted and noted that he did not have me report to the Hospital Commander and give a personal account of the details of this fellow physician's/officer's death. I had nothing for or against my CO (commanding officer), but I considered his handling of the death of this soldier more one of embarrassment than sorrow.

It was my daily habit to cross the road in front of the hospital compound at day's end, go into and through the Korean village, making my way to a bare hill on the west side of this village. Up the hill, I would go, arriving at the top where there was a large shell crater, or perhaps, more likely, a former gun emplacement, probably an artillery position.

Korea had beautiful sunsets, and as almost all roads were dirt, and with there being a large volume of military vehicular traffic, creating much dust in the air, this, in turn, contributed to the vivid colors.

So upon this hill, I repaired at the end of the workday for personal devotional time. Taking my New Testament and hymnbook, though I never could sing worth a flip, not modesty here, but honesty, I read the scripture for a time, meditated and had prayer, and then read aloud the words of the grand old hymns of my Christian faith.

Medical Detachment, 1st Medical Field Laboratory, Detachment C.O., Frank Glenn Marsh, 1st Lt. MSC 121st Evacuation Hospital, Yong Dong Po, Korea, 22 June 1953

Passing in Review, Outgoing and Incoming 8th US Army Surgeons, 1st Medical Field Laboratory, Frank G. Marsh, 1st Lt. MSC, Detachment Commander, S/Sgt. William L. Sluss, Guidon Bearer, 121st Evacuation Hospital, Yong Dong Po, Korea, 22 June 1953

I lingered as the beautiful sunset, previously referred to, bathed the hilltop in that distinctive ever-changing pattern of light until darkness came upon me. Then I made my way back to my bunk in the Quonset hut.

No more meals, conversation, or hiking to the shower with Jim – ever.

It was a great day, a truly joyful day for all, when helicopters began bringing in our repatriated prisoners of war. In addition to their return, the truce having been signed, we knew we would be going home soon. I had one R&R (rest and recuperation) visit to Japan during my Korean tour of duty where I had a great reunion with Donna and Virgil McMillan, ex-Auburn students, who were then Baptist missionaries in Japan. Another great reunion occurred with Leroy Robinson, my best friend at Auburn during college days. He was in the counterintelligence corps (CIC) and cautioned me not to mention that as my destination, but rather to give his address only. I hailed a cab and followed Leroy's instructions. The cab driver broke into a big smile, and said, "Ah, so, CIC!!"

Leroy Robinson, best friend from college days at Auburn, and Glenn in Tokyo, Japan, 1953

John Lowery, Glenn, and Don Pipkin with F-86 Fighter aircraft, the type flown by John in Korea, 1953

Co. A 81st Medium Tank Battalion, Ft. Chaffee, Arkansas, where Army odyssey began and ended. Picture taken on way home from Korea, December 1953

Wedding picture, Glenn and Elisabeth Ann Stadnick, First Baptist Church, Bakersfield, California, December 8, 1953

The Marsh boys (l to r), Ralph W. (oldest), Albert G. (our father), Leon (second oldest), Glenn (youngest). Auburn, Alabama, Christmas, 1953. Photo courtesy of Dr. Leon Marsh

The troop ship, *Maritime Phoenix*, arrived in Seattle in early December 1953, and I took a train to California. The Cascades were snow laden and unbelievably beautiful as we passed through that mountain range. I went to Bakersfield, California, picked up my car, and as I tell it, when I pulled out of the Pipkin's driveway on the way to pick up Elisabeth, who was flying to Los Angeles to meet me, I looked in the rear view mirror, and all I could see were teeth from my gigantic smile. Home at last. I knew what time Elisabeth was to arrive, but not the airline, so I drove to various air terminals, as the airport was arranged in those days, until I came to the correct one, We drove back to the Pipkins, and the next day, purchased rings, obtained our marriage license, and were married at the First Baptist Church of Bakersfield. All the people we knew in Bakersfield were there, the pastor and four members of the Pipkin family. We left immediately for Fort Chaffee, Arkansas for separation from the Army. It is ironic that the Army journey began and ended at the same place. Out of the Army, at last, we arrived in Auburn a few days before Christmas 1953.

GRADUATE SCHOOL IN PHARMACOLOGY

AT AUBURN

Beginning graduate school in January 1954, I received a Master of Science degree in Pharmacy in the spring of 1955 from Auburn and was elected to Phi Kappa Phi. An addition to the faculty at the Auburn School of Pharmacy was B. B. Williams, PhD. What a scholar, teacher, and gentleman he was – one of the three greatest teachers I had – ever (as noted in the section dealing with my three greatest professors).

Professor Hargreaves was on my graduate committee and renewing my friendship with him was rewarding as I continued my interest in Pharmaceutical Chemistry, his particular area of expertise.

Emory University Graduate School, 1958

Our first child, a daughter, Elisabeth Ann, was born on a Saturday morning, October 23, 1954. I believe it to be the first and only time I missed going to my Saturday job, moonlighting as a pharmacist in Lanette, Alabama, where I made several delightful friends. As a means to hold the family together financially, I was gainfully employed in other part-time jobs as well. One such job was not so pleasant as it involved

*Ann fishing with her Dad. Photo taken February 23, 1957
at a pond outside Atlanta, Georgia*

cleaning the cages of rats used in experiments; however, I did enjoy my third job, which was grading the laboratory assignments for Professor Joe Rash.

Upon receiving my Master of Science degree from Auburn, I made application to graduate school at Emory University seeking a PhD. degree in Pharmacology.

AT EMORY

After an exhaustive exam, I was admitted to advanced standing at Emory Graduate School in the fall of 1955. I muddled through two years of academic work often in the same classes as medical students with whom I felt much in common, while what little research I did was of little consequence. Most of all, I did not like being isolated in a research laboratory away from other people and reached the point of dreading entering the laboratory. After much soul searching, I applied to medical school at Emory, and was accepted. I was then immediately in my element. I've never regretted the change, only regretted my limited adaptability to research earlier.

During this interval, our first son, John Leon, was born April 13, 1957 and missed, by only five days, being born on his Grandfather Marsh's birthday.

As an interested student of human nature and as with my previous educational experiences, I observed and mentally catalogued the eccentricities of many of my professors and friends at Emory as well as the humorous episodes I experienced there.

Following are some of the more notable memories:

HARRY WILLIAMS, MD

Harry Williams was my favorite basic sciences professor at Emory Medical School. He was in the Navy in WW II, went back to high school and graduated, then entered college achieving a degree in pre-med, then a degree in medicine. He had an absolute gift insofar as relating to people was concerned.

Sadly, pancreatic cancer took his life prematurely, but his name lives on, as a medical school lecture hall was named in his honor.

He also had a great fund of stories. This is my favorite: A farmer bought a prize-winning bull, but the bull preferred to eat grass rather than do what came naturally. In an over-the-fence discussion, the bull's owner related the problem to his farmer neighbor. The neighbor suggested a consultation with the new veterinarian in town. The owner of the bull was not convinced, and the two did not see each other again for several weeks.

When again they met, the owner of the bull was ecstatic, relating that all of his cows were with calf, and the bull had jumped the fence to visit another neighbor's heifers.

The neighbor who had suggested the veterinarian was much surprised and asked, "What did the vet give that bull?"

The owner said, "I don't know, but it tastes like peppermint."

Mentally Deficient (MD) and Piled higher and Deeper (PhD)

When I was in graduate school at Emory, the chairman of one of the departments had both PhD and MD degrees. From observing him, I came close to reaching the conclusion that having both of these degrees just about extirpates all of one's allotment of common sense; at least, this was the case for him.

Another graduate student, Frode Ulvedahl, and I were taking a course in Radioisotope Techniques by this professor, and early in the course, he began touting a trip to the V. A. Hospital to observe their procedures.

While the new V. A. Hospital is much closer to Emory than was the old V. A., this "old" V. A. was still no more than five, or so miles away, but one would think, listening to him, that we were going to the Rockefeller Institute. Seems like two or three times a week, we'd hear about the upcoming trip to the V. A.

Finally, he announced that we'd be going to this facility the next day, further announcing that we'd go in the other student's car since I walked to class, or in his car, but in an aside to my fellow student, he assured him that should we go in his – the student's car, he, the MD/PhD would buy Frode some gasoline. Now, this professor, chairman of the department had two cars, one a family sedan, one of the last Packards made, which looked like an old-fashioned, upside-down bath tub, and the other, a sports car, single seat affair. On the days he drove the sports car, so as to appear dashing, he added a tweed cap and a scarf to his usual attire.

Well, the big day came. Our professor arrived in his sports car, thus making the decision that we would be traveling in Frode's Olds 88, 1954 model. However, our leader assured Frode that yes, indeed, we would stop either coming or going to get that gas. So off we went to the V. A., and it was mentioned, at least one more time, as we arrived at the V. A. that getting the gas was the number one priority on the way back to Emory. We spent, probably, an hour and a half there, and as we pulled out of the parking lot, the subject of buying gas came up again.

As we motored along, our leader sitting in the back seat, quite erect with arms folded, upon spying a service station, almost shouted, "There's one; there's where I'm going to get you the gas. Pull in!"

We did. In a matter of seconds, in those days before pumping one's own gas was heard of, the attendant was at the driver's window. "Fill 'er up?" he asked.

I had noticed the gasoline prices posted to be thirty-one and a half cents per gallon for regular and thirty-three and a half cents for ethyl.

Frode didn't answer, but our leader said, "No, two gallons, please."

The attendant asked, "Regular or ethyl?" Now, an Olds 88 ran on high test, as it was called in those days, but Frode, though being from Norway, still knew a cheapskate when he saw one. When he heard, "Two gallons," and also with his mind probably influenced by the fact that a grade in the course would be forthcoming, swallowed hard and said, "Regular."

As the gas was being pumped, our thrifty professor rolled down his window and magnanimously said, "Make that sixty-five cents worth," two cents greater than the original order.

The gas pumper, able to contain himself no longer, facetiously asked, "You all goin' to Florida?"

Our leader with all his education never realized it was not a genuine question, but rather a reference to his tight fist, said, "No, we're just going back to Emory."

I bit the inside of my lips until they bled to hold in the laughter. For a long time, this was the funniest thing I had ever witnessed. Somehow without exploding, I did control my laughter until we reached his parking place back on campus. I excused myself and walking as fast as I could, reached the corner of the nearest building where I turned out of their sight and collapsed against the building in gales of uncontrolled, near hysteric laughter.

Only then did I realize what our leader meant, when after devouring from cover to cover a new issue of *Life* magazine commented, "This is a good magazine, but twenty cents is too much!"

In a sense, we two students had the last laugh. He took a position elsewhere and we were relieved.

IMPERSONATOR

Most Auburn people tolerate football even if they don't love it. Those that love it are the majority. I missed it and when in Emory graduate school, needed a football "fix" in the worst way. Now, I would have loved to have seen an Auburn game, but was so deprived of Southeastern Conference football, just any conference game would suffice.

In our church there was a grandmother, who on very rare occasions, when we could afford her modest charge, babysat for us. Her son had been an Atlanta city bus driver. It was customary at Grant Field, Georgia Tech's football stadium, to allow the bus drivers transporting fans to the game to have standing room only privileges during the game.

My criminal mind saw this courtesy as an opportunity to go to a real live football game, as we did not have TV. I borrowed the son's uniform and without bus, entered the stadium area, then through the gates and followed the real drivers to "our area." They knew somehow that I wasn't one of them, and many watched me more than the game. I think they believed me to be some sort of bus company official observing the comportment of the drivers.

As I recall, I left quite early, never feeling at ease in a gate-crasher role.

MEDICAL SCHOOL

In fall 1958, I entered medical school, joining the sophomores as the oldest student in the class. Since the GI bill had run out at about this time, I was truly on my own. I was a member of the US Army Reserves, 158th General Hospital, with rank as Captain. This helped especially in summer when I drew active duty pay for two weeks at summer camp. I also worked one summer at the V.A. Hospital doing research, which was incorporated into an ongoing study, the results of which were published, but I don't remember where.

With the Help of a Friend
Emmett Mashburn

The summer break at Emory was then reduced from three months to one month for medical school students, so summer employment was no longer a viable option. At some point, I went to work at North Decatur Pharmacy as I was licensed to practice pharmacy in Georgia. I am unable to remember my starting pay, but about one year later, I was offered a job for more money as a pharmacist, $2.50 per hour. The job was, however, farther away from Emory. My employer matched the offer, and I stayed on, working the schedule opposite a pharmacist who had been employed there for a long time. This worked rather well except in my senior year, I believe it was, when I was on a rotation that caused me to work every third rather than every other or every fourth night. Because the pharmacist working opposite me would not agree to work four extra hours, with pay, of course, over a two-week period in order to accommodate my new rotation sequence, I was forced to take a leave of absence. However, Emmett Mashburn, the day pharmacist, in contradistinction, was so kind as to pick up my shift and hold the fort, that is pharmacy, until my rotation changed in six weeks or so. I borrowed money to live on during this time. Emmett and his wife Charlotte deserve much credit for their support. Not only was he willing to do this, but upon my return to work, when I, sometimes had to return, unexpectedly to the hospital, or not be able to leave the hospital to be on time for work, he would, without hesitation, cover for me until I could get there. He is deceased now, but I owe him a great debt of gratitude for his unfailing allegiance in those terribly difficult times. Thank you, my true friend.

Life at Emory University in Atlanta was in a word – difficult. I had a wife and two children with a third born during my third year of medical school, and no financial base. I often found myself in the situation of needing to be three different places at the same time. Insofar as I know, the only thing that was truly unique in my situation was that I held essentially a full-time job and attended medical school at the same time. Inasmuch as outside jobs were strictly prohibited for medical students, and the pharmacy was near Emory where a member of the faculty might come into the store at anytime, I developed a keen eye and kept a close watch on the door, so that I might duck out of sight and not be found out.

MY BLACK BAG

At the beginning of the second year of medical school, the black bags that we medical students had ordered arrived. We would not be using them very much initially, as it turned out, mainly for the course in physical diagnosis as we were, at this stage, much occupied with didactic studies of biochemistry, bacteriology, now microbiology, among others.

I remember unpacking the bag, opening and closing it over and over, listening to the reassuring snap of the closure. Next, I placed in the bag the blood pressure cuff and accompanying stethoscope, then the combination otoscope/ophthalmoscope, complete with attachments, and finally the reflex hammer. I felt like I was going to be a real doctor, and I was self-conscious about the smile that I had difficulty suppressing as I walked home, crossing the Emory campus on the way, and hoping that my neophyte status was not obvious.

That black bag became a part of me over the next few years, but its contents were not limited to instruments. It was a favorite repository while I was in medical school for a brown bag containing a sandwich and most importantly of all, a place to smuggle a *Synopsis of Pathology*, the common sense size of the giant tome, *Textbook of Pathology* written by Anderson. The chairman of Department of Pathology was incensed to catch a student substituting the small for the large. This was the same person who utilized the ploy of telling the top student (or two) in the class during their oral pathology exam that they had done poorly and would be re-examined. One can only imagine the ripple effect this had on the remainder of the class when they heard this, and then wondered what chance they, the lesser-ranked students had to pass.

Ernie Abernathy was one year ahead of me in medical school and had an experience with Dr. Sheldon worth repeating. When Ernie had just finished his grueling, oral pathology exam, in a tension relieving attempt, he remarked, "Dr. Sheldon, I guess they could write a book about what I don't know about pathology."

As quickly as a cat pouncing upon a mouse, Dr. Sheldon replied in his thick German accent, "Zey have already. Ze name of ze book is Anderson!"

Medical school was initially an exhilarating experience for me, as I desired to be a "real doctor" more than anything. The term "real doctor" was in contradistinction to PhD which some regarded as a "paper doctor" or "teaching doctor." Medical school was also a frustrating experience with my having to earn a living, such as it was, at the same time while placing serious restraints on my time for study with this responsibility not shared by any other member of the class. I was home one evening, one week and two evenings, alternate weeks. In addition to my shift as a pharmacist at a nearby drugstore, I was also on duty and on call at the hospital, and had Army reserve meetings some evenings, and camp for two weeks in the summers as well. This posed quite a handicap when competing with my classmates, who for the most part, had little or no financial worries, and could, thus, devote themselves to study.

Not only was the paucity of time a serious handicap, but also there was a real constriction on funds for textbooks. I derived a scheme to overcome, with the help of my classmates, this problem and was able to have access to the necessary books. First, I would determine the book or books necessary for a given course and check them out from the medical school library prior to the beginning of the course and then renew the withdrawal the number of times permitted. After the last renewal permitted, a classmate who owned the requisite book would accompany me as I returned the book and saying something like, "I've been waiting for this book," he would check it out, then after we left the library, hand it to me. He then would renew the book the permitted number of times. Then at the end of that time, I would accompany him to the library, check out the book under my own name and, of course, renew the withdrawal again. In this way, I had access to the texts without having to purchase them which otherwise would have been impossible. With this "baling wire" approach holding my educational experience together, I often wondered how I stacked up knowledge-wise with the other students, especially those whom I knew to be in the upper tier, academically.

In the wee hours of the night when I was teamed with the number one or number two ranked student in the class, I boldly made my observations known saying, "Jim, I know you are ranked number one or number two in the class, and I've been observing you, and I find that there's not a nickel's worth of difference in what I know and what you know."

He then said, "I've been observing you too, and you're right."

In addition to the feeling of accomplishment gained at that time by this acknowledgment, I have, over the years, admired and respected the candor of Jim Spann, the other student. This illustrates the cohesion of the class of '61 Emory University School of Medicine still noted at our reunion in 1996.

Somewhere about the middle of my junior year in medical school, one of my professors, Dr. Huguley, broached the subject of some sort of financial aid for me. I didn't pursue what information he had or the source of this information, but I told him that I was getting by and that unless there were a health problem or some sort of unexpected disaster, I should be able to make it financially. I further suggested that there might be someone in the class in more restrictive financial straits than was I and thus, more deserving. He discounted that and bluntly said, "We have the money in a student loan fund and you should take it." I did, and thus, thankfully I had these funds to sustain my family when the already-mentioned scheduling difficulty at the drugstore arose.

MISS WELLBORN

Miss Wellborn was elderly and had lived with her sister for a number of years, but when I met her, her sister had recently died and she lived alone. Though I was a senior medical student and she an elderly patient, we "took to each other," with her looking forward to my visits and my looking forward to seeing her each day of her lengthy hospital stay. I had a knack for drawing blood and could usually find a vein even in the most obese or obscure-veined persons. Maybe that's what she liked about me, as I never had to stick her but once.

Early one morning as I came into her room, I found her in a "tizzy," as were the nurses. There had been numerous unsuccessful attempts at venapuncture, and in a fit of temper, she had bounced a bedpan off the door to her room. Well, she calmed down. So did I, and as providence would have it, I obtained the blood needed on the first try. We were friends for life, which regrettably, was not very long. She crocheted a doily for my wife for Christmas, and once, when I attended a medical meeting in South Carolina, I detoured on the way home by way of Atlanta just to visit her in a nursing home. What a welcome, befitting a mid-eastern prince! We exchanged Christmas cards and occasional letters for a few years until one of those cards was returned after Christmas marked, "Deceased." I remember fondly her kind smile and the way she made me feel special.

As one might expect, family excursions were limited both by funds and time. Occasionally, we'd go to a drive-in theater for one dollar per carload, and for a real splurge, we'd visit Horton's, a hamburger place just off the Emory campus. I can remember money being exquisitely short, to the point that a quarter left over from grocery necessities would go for a six-pack of Cokes. On one of these occasions when the groceries had been put away and the budget had allowed the carton of Cokes, we opened one of those 6 1/2 oz. "elixirs of delight" and poured it over ice cubes for daughter Ann, aged four or five. As she hastily raised the glass, the effervescence went up her nose and into her eyes and with reddened eyes and tears of joy, she exclaimed, "I'm just wild about sody." Talk about a missed Coca Cola photo op!

When it comes to memories, my trunks are full. I'm a multimillionaire!

Ann was fortunate to have a cousin from whom she received clothes, as they were outgrown. Her cousin's bicycle, repaired, became her first bike. Since one could buy spare shoe soles at the dime store in those days, my having my grandfather's shoe last allowed me to half-sole shoes as needed. My mother had an uncanny ability to purchase and mail dresses for Ann that always fit, despite the fact that she didn't see Ann very often.

JESUS COUNT

In the days before the pill, medical students delivered a lot of babies, especially being on the delivery suite 12 hours on and 12 hours off, seven-days-a-week for three weeks.

I learned to doze on a litter and do what I called a Jesus count. By listening to the frequency and intensity of the patient's supplications to "Jesus"–"Lord Jesus"–"Sweet Jesus," I could determine, with little error, when it was time to proceed from labor room to delivery room. Not once was I late, only early a few times.

Working those long hours without adequate sleep could cause me to be a bit "slap-happy." In one of those somewhat manic, sleep-deprived times, I said to the patient in labor, "Having a baby is not near as much fun as making it, is it?" She replied, "That's the Lord's truth, that's the Lord's truth!"

No quarter was asked or given, and the faculty was demanding, often to excess and sometimes mean-spirited. Students had no rights in those days, our consolation being in camaraderie with classmates and self-reliance only. As an example, a classmate and I were on duty when the following exchange took place.

The faculty member came onto the hospital ward about 7:00 a.m. for rounds. He inquired of my fellow student why blood had not been drawn for a certain laboratory study ordered. This student replied that he had not had time, explaining that late admissions and patient work-ups that night had kept us up until about 3:30 a.m., and we were up again at 5:30 a.m. drawing blood.

When asked how many meals he had had during the past 24 hours, the student replied, "One in the hospital cafeteria, a

Coke and pack of crackers for another, and the third missed entirely because of lack of time."

The faculty member in the coldest, most inhumane, sarcastic tone I have ever heard replied, "You had plenty of time to take care of this patient. You chose to spend all of your time eating and sleeping!"

There were many other similar incidents.

The end result of this was night terrors, always concerning my status as medical student. That, and the fear of failure as a recurrent theme has persisted to the present, though now more than 40 years, not as frequent. Interestingly, at the reunion of the class of 1961, five years ago, the above was a commonly related experience. My view in retrospect was that what should have been the educational experience of a lifetime, was flawed or marred by too many on the faculty who seemed to feel that terror was a normal means of teaching.

While I always looked for the humor in any and all situations, there were times when that commodity was hard to come by. On one surgery rotation where it was common to go into the operating room at 7:00 a.m. and not get out until 12 hours later, with no chance for toilet, food, or other breaks, and then with the daytime admissions still waiting for work-up, humor was, indeed, scarce.

Even then, I remember a patient who returned a few days after hospital discharge with dehiscence (separation) of his surgical wound. What a mess! When I asked him what had happened, he reminded me that the opening day of quail season occurred a few days after his hospital discharge.

I said, "You didn't go hunting!"

He replied, "Sure did and got my limit too."

I had to laugh with him, and found his exuberance refreshing. One student, his name, now long forgotten, did get in his digs on this rotation, directed at the chief of service. As mentioned, the surgical procedure went on for hours, and the medical student had, but two functions, to hold the retractors exposing the surgical field and the other to endure, silently all the abuse, both verbal and sometimes physical, forceps across knuckles, elbowing and kicks these surgeons wished to dish out. During this three-week rotation, I was never taught nor shown any anatomical feature. My situation was not unique, but typical.

At the hospital in those days, one could look out the OR window and see the azaleas and camellias growing and blooming with great profusion in springtime. On this occasion, likened to the last dog in the sled team, being able to see only asses, in this case someone else's elbows, he was viewing the botanical wonders through the windows when this profane chief roundly cursed him and ended his tirade with this statement, "Get your *blankety-blank* mind on what we are doing; the *blankety-blank* trees and flowers will be there when we get through."

The student replied, "Yes, Dr. Fisk, but they won't be green."

Another story dealing with the harsh treatment by the faculty on surgery rotation was related to me one night when I was working in the pharmacy. Dr. Thompson, a local pediatrician, came in. He asked me what rotation I was on, and when I replied a surgery rotation, he said, "Oh, my." He then asked me if I knew Dr. Johnson, a local chest surgeon.

I said, "Yes," and he said, "Let me tell you what I saw happen to him when he was an intern and I was a senior student on that rotation. This doctor, referred to, did something that Dr. Fisk did not like, and so as punishment, he was made to stand near an IV stand and multiple rolls of surgical tape were wrapped around him and the IV stand. Appearing as a subject about to be burned at the stake, he was not set afire, but rather, he was subjected to a full tray of surgical instruments being poured over his (intern's) head." These long ago, but memorable events surely are no longer tolerated by anyone, and shouldn't be.

I noticed over the years that while patients complained about long waiting time to see the doctor, and on occasion complained about the bill, the number one complaint, in reference to doctors, was, "The doctor just doesn't listen to me." While I have numerous and valid complaints about my medical education, we *were*, nonetheless, taught to listen and to observe. As applied to medicine, listening to what the patient said often revealed the diagnosis, or at least, formed the basis for appropriate investigative studies that would provide the diagnosis.

Dr. Oliver Wendell Holmes, a pioneer along with Sir William Osler in scientific medicine, stressed listening and observing as invaluable tools in physical diagnosis.

As the story goes, Dr. Holmes presented a patient to his class of medical students. This patient had diabetes, and he reminded the students that her kidneys were spilling sugar that was then excreted in her urine. Near the patient was a bottle of urine, which he assured the students, was, in fact, voided by this particular patient. He, however, said that they should determine for themselves that this patient with diabetes had sugar in her urine. By touching the tip of their index finger to the urine and by tasting, they could verify this. The students dutifully filed by following their teacher, touched their index finger to the urine, thence to their tongue as Dr. Holmes had instructed and thus followed his example.

Dr. Holmes then made his point, reminding them of his admonition to be both good listeners and observers. They had listened to Dr. Holmes, but alas, had fallen short on observation as he pointed out he had touched the urine with his index finger, but used his middle finger to touch his tongue.

Along with listening, there is implied the asking of the correct questions in the medical history. Questions should, in certain instances, go beyond medicine. The most striking example of this abrogation of responsibility concerns the surgical removal of a patient's tongue at another university hospital. Only after surgery was it discovered that the patient was illiterate. Not knowing all of the facts, it may not have been possible to utilize another modality (radiation) for treatment of his cancer, but this information should have been known pre-operatively.

Sir William Osler reportedly said, "To study medicine without books is like a ship without a rudder; to study medicine without patients is not to go to sea at all."

Dr. Scarborough

While Emory was noted for its medical facilities and its faculty, very few of us in the class of '61 were beneficiaries of a kind word or encouragement of any kind. In fact, after graduation, completion of internship and residency, and opening a practice in Lexington, Kentucky and appointment to the University of Kentucky Medical School faculty on a voluntary basis, I decided that I would, as best I could, eschew the Emory way and do the opposite, as far as teaching was concerned.

A notable exception to the above criticism was Dr. Scarborough, an excellent physician, surgeon, and a kind, compassionate human being with a sense of humor. When a senior rotating through the Winship Clinic, I had Dr. Scarborough as teacher. Dr. Scarborough's teaching technique included the student's seeing the patient, doing the medical history and appropriate medical exam, followed by the student's preliminary diagnosis. Dr. Scarborough would then have the student present the case orally, after which, Dr. Scarborough would himself go into the examination room, review the history, perform his own physical exam, arrive at his own diagnosis, and then discuss the patient in detail with the student. He was a marvelous teacher and role model.

At the conclusion of the discussion, the student would return to the patient, set into motion the management/treatment plan for the patient, and dictate the same, including history and physical exam, for inclusion in the patient's chart. The student, at least this one, could not help but emulate Dr. Scarborough in many ways, sometimes including his language. He had a habit of using the word *fatigueability*. I picked up on that and made mention in the record as to whether the patient had increased fatigueability or not. One morning, as clinic was beginning, the secretary challenged me, informing me that there was no such word as *fatigueability*, at least, not listed in the dictionary. Hearing Dr. Scarborough's approaching footsteps, I was seized with an act of bravado that could have, with some (maybe most) of the faculty, been a one-way ticket out of medical school. As he came within earshot, I replied, "The dictionary must be wrong. Dr. Scarborough uses that word, and he's a graduate of the University of Alabama, and those people are never wrong about anything."

With a hint of a smile, he said as he passed, "The best defense is a good offense." Only then realizing what I had done, I breathed a sigh of relief and went back to the straight and narrow path, which I was expected to follow as a medical student. Years later, Dr. Scarborough succumbed to cancer, the disease he had fought so intensely in the lives of his patients.

Should I be forced to choose just one person on the faculty, who, in my own vision and romantic notion, fully met my idea of an ideal physician, it would have been Dr. Scarborough.

CONFERENCE CALL

When I was a senior medical student in the days before the pill, there was little if any sleep on the Ob-Gyn rotation. On this one night, actually, about 3:30 in the a.m., there were no deliveries in progress, and the Chief Resident summoned those on service to a conference. Present, in addition to the Chief Resident, were the Senior Resident, Junior Resident, Intern, and myself.

When we were seated, and with the Chief Resident presiding, we were asked to relate, in turn, the most embarrassing experience that we had ever had. I don't remember any of the experiences related, mine included, but when the Chief Resident's turn came (he was last), it went something like this, and is definitely memorable.

His fraternity at the University of Florida had a formal dinner with a certain sorority as guests. The menu was roast beef, mashed potatoes, gravy, green peas, salad, rolls, and dessert. At this point, we were asked if we had ever had a sudden, unexpected, without warning, explosive sneeze. Of course, we all had. He continued asking us to picture this – ill at ease fraternity brothers in their tuxes with their dates in formal gowns with corsages. They had been seated and are just starting to eat. Our speaker had a fork loaded with peas entering his mouth, when this ol' devil sneeze occurred without warning. Achew! The peas sprayed forth fanning out over the table–that is, all except one pea, which suspended by a *snotcicle,* swung gently back and forth. He then said all one could hear was the sound of chairs being pushed away from the table. Dinner was over.

I wish I still knew this doctor's name as I have, for these many years, told this story which has brought so much laughter to so many people, and I would just like to thank him. I also admire one who can tell such a self-deflating experience.

Your Wish is My Command

One of the really major hurdles to overcome at Emory Medical School was to get through the surgery rotation. The chairman of General Surgery was Dr. J. D. Martin, a true gentleman. Always interested in students, he conducted on Sunday morning, a session during one's rotation on this service that was referred to as "Sunday school." This renowned surgeon furnished coffee and doughnuts, and the subjects discussed included the general topics of medical interest such as famous early physicians, philosophy of medicine, and the ethics of medicine.

Once during rotation on his service, at the end of his lecture, he assigned me a topic on a very obscure facet of medicine. In his offhanded way he said something like, "Marsh, see what you can find on the cause of death of the U.S. presidents dying in office, excluding assassination, and tell us about it next time."

I set about this task and could find absolutely nothing about it in either of the two medical libraries to which I had access. I was prepared to say just that, and on the day my report was due, I was in surgery clinic, which preceded the lecture hour. A fellow student asked me what I had to report. I replied, "Nothing, and I'm going to say so."

His wise counsel was to say that I had better have something to say on some subject, so arranging for fellow students to see those patients that I ordinarily would have seen, I beat a hasty path to the library in an absolute state of panic. A book on a frontier doctor in the American West caught my eye. I read the whole book in about 45 minutes, the remaining clinic time and lunchtime. When called upon, allowed as how I could find little to report on the assigned subject, but I had something else. I was allowed to proceed and wowed my classmates with nearly an hour on the subject of frontier medical practice. The chief called me a raconteur (I didn't even know what that meant at the time), invited me at the end of class to his office and presented me with a copy of his latest paper that had been published. I did affirm that necessity is, indeed, the mother of invention, and that panic is a great motivator. Also, not lost on me was that a wish from the faculty should be interpreted as a command.

One Saturday afternoon in the fall of my senior year, my pharmacist friend Emmett Mashburn and I worked all afternoon on my 1954 Ford. The results were some improvement but not dramatic. The car limped along and near the end of my senior year, it gave out. I had spent money on it that I could not afford, only to have something else go wrong. I was bumming rides from Emory to Grady Hospital, and with no certain way to get to work at the drugstore, things were in crisis. Internship had been assigned; "matching" is what they call it, and I had received what I had hoped for, an Army internship at Fitzsimons General Hospital in Denver, Colorado. I had to have an internship that paid a living wage. Fact! An internship at Emory-Grady Hospital paid $55 monthly, duty was every other night, two, not three, meals daily in the hospital cafeteria were provided and also laundering of uniforms. That sounded like involuntary servitude to me, and I did desire to keep my wife and three children, and having already been in the Army three years, I knew what it would be like. The pay would allow for a better standard of living than I was used to, and I would not have to go into debt any further. Besides, the Assistant Chief of Medicine at Emory had been a career Army medical officer and I liked and trusted him, and when he assured me that I would receive a quality learning experience, I enlisted his help. No doubt, he helped me a great deal, and while I wrote to him from time to time, when I called on him on a few occasions, I always seemed to miss him. I admired him greatly as a man and as a teacher. Dr. Garland Herndon later became director of the Emory Winship Clinic.

So with proof of internship in hand, I marched down to the Emory branch of the Citizens and Southern Bank to obtain a loan to buy a car, but no collateral, no deal. I really felt defeated when victory seemed so near. I called my mother (my father had been dead about one year) and asked her to call our family banker of many years, Mr. Emil Wright, president of the Bank of Auburn. A stipulation of the loan request by me was that a co-signer would not be needed. If my signature were not enough, I'd walk. Tough talk for a walking pauper, but Mr. Wright understood. He told Mother to tell me to pick out what I wanted. I chose a Ford Falcon station wagon, their cheapest offered, no air conditioner or other non-necessities, and somehow I got the old car to Auburn where I traded it in on the new one. I always thought it ironic that my mother's ophthalmologist was Dr. Emil Wright Jr. and her dermatologist-son's savior banker was Mr. Emil Wright Sr.

With two children, and the third, David Glenn, born May 11, 1960, the week of my father's death, the age-old tradition of professional courtesy, now all but gone, served us well. The pediatricians and obstetrician, Armand Hendee, MD, were helpful beyond words. We kept use of medical services to an absolute minimum, but their gracious rendering of services is still remembered. I learned a lesson from this. Never, never did I ever charge other physicians or any member of their immediate families. I did not even charge their children until they finished graduate school if they decided to go that far.

JACK IN THE BOX

We had, during Internal Medicine rotation at Grady Hospital, what was referred to by the students as "Jack in the Box" rounds, which was basically two hours of terror. On Thursday mornings, we would assemble in the conference room with either the Chief or Assistant Chief of Medicine conducting the session. It would start off pleasantly enough, on the surface, by the one in charge asking, "Who has patient so-and-so?"

Sounds reasonable so far, but the problem already before one was to decide, at that precise moment, if that was one of "yours" or one of "theirs," the other students on service. Realize, however, that each student, on average, had up to two dozen assigned patients with admission and discharges occurring every day. The questioner had the patient's chart in hand and knew who was assigned to that patient. Assuming the patient was "yours," it was then your responsibility to present the complete medical scenario in intimate detail, without notes, i.e. the date of onset of symptoms, the nature of these symptoms, the family medical history, the individual's past medical history, previous medication, and then the physical exam including the head, eyes, ears, nose, throat, chest, lungs, and heart, abdomen, and genitourinary. Then one was expected to know the precise results of the laboratory findings – normal or abnormal was unacceptable. One was also expected to give diagnosis. The preliminary diagnosis was often called *working diagnosis*.

Bear in mind, the Chief could, and did, interrupt at any time, forcing one to defend any decision or plan of treatment made. Interruption was often by negative comment or question, and survival of the session was exhausting.

On the morning of these sessions, I would arrive at the hospital hours beforehand to re-prepare. The usual consensus

Glenn and Elisabeth, Medical School graduation, June, 1961

among the students was that the sessions were like shooting fish in a barrel, and we were the fish.

One of my classmates, V. W. L., who died just last year, thought it one of his crowning accomplishments of medical school that he was a senior, and that the Chief of Medicine did not recognize him. Anonymity was desirable, not too good to be point man, and tail-end Charlie position, not at all recommended. There was considerable merit to being in the middle of the pack.

On one of those winter mornings, when I left early to finish "preparation" for this ordeal, the dirt, actually, mud, road leading from where we lived on Andrew Circle to the main street,

Clifton Road, which bisected Emory University campus, had received, during the night, considerable rain, and I found myself stuck in the mud. After quite a long time, I was able to be extricated, made it back home, out of that muddy white uniform and shoes and after another shower, started all over again, with reduced preparation time and the gnawing panic of not being completely prepared. I was fortunate not to be called upon that day. Whew!

As I write this, 2002, a vestige of the anxiety and terror comes back to me. The reader is apt to say, "It couldn't be that bad." It wasn't – it was worse. I had nightmares for many years, as often as two or three times a month, at first, but gradually and slowly decreasing, till now, occurring but two to three times yearly.

Some of the best sleep I have ever gotten has been within the last ten years after awakening panic stricken as a result of a night terror about medical school, then fully realizing that I have not only graduated, but also have retired from my practice, I then drifted into peaceful sleep.

Once when returning to Emory for a medical conference, as we stood in that same long hallway waiting to go in to see a patient, my classmate D. D. said to me, "Getting through this place was Hell." I agreed wholeheartedly.

In both the class before mine, as well as in my own graduating class, a member of each class with only three to four months to go, was told that he would not graduate. What does one do with seven years plus of pre-med and medical school? He does not practice medicine.

The member of my class, E. G., who did not graduate just wasn't with us toward the end of our senior year. Rumor has it, that after he learned that he would not graduate, he took his life.

The Chairman of Ob-Gyn told my mother at my graduation, "The record won't show it, but Glenn is an honor student. He had to be, to maintain his work schedule and perform academically." I had no idea that he knew of my circumstances and his comment was much appreciated.

After graduation, which was somewhat saddened by the absence of my father, we headed west, stopping off in Auburn to see my family and in St. Louis to see Elisabeth's family. Moving day was quite a scene. When we had started housekeeping in January 1954, we had bought a new two-piece bedroom suite, a new Hotpoint refrigerator, which came from Jake Hitchcock's next to Markle's Drug in Auburn, and a new gas range that came from the gas place on North College Street. Everything else was extreme hand-me-down, hand-cobbled kitchen hanging cabinets from fruit crates, repainted, used baby beds, worn out toys, bookcases made from concrete blocks and 1 X 12 pine boards, and our living room easy chair and matching sofa for which we had paid a total of $25. Some of our stuff we had because we had beaten the trash pickup crew to our neighbor's curbside. The base cabinet in the kitchen had been purchased from a neighbor a year or two before when they moved, so it went along and became my workbench for years. Whenever we moved, it moved, and today it is still my workbench. You really must understand that this was Emory housing and the kitchen came complete with two outlets, not one cabinet in the kitchen, but a couple of homemade shelves were under the hanging sink. Everything we had was well used but thought needed and we looked like the 49ers headed west except the Army provided a van instead of a covered wagon.

When the movers closed the van door and pulled away, we took a last look at our home after six years of trial and tribulation and finally triumph! Was it worth it? You bet it was! Now Andrew Circle is no more, nor is the small Emory Post office with our box # 67. I have been back several times to the former location of 39 Andrew Circle, and I can recognize the site because of the still standing trees now much larger and the honeysuckle still growing on the school fence where I planted it as a privacy screen. Bitter-sweet memories of sacrifice by both of us – all night study sessions with panic (the great anti-sleep motivator), weariness beyond words (once falling asleep while eating), kids' first words, sick kids (with no money for doctors, if they charged), no money for a wristwatch (until I absolutely had to have it for taking pulse and respiration counts), Christmases with my drugstore bonus of $25 given to my wife for her present, another Christmas with wife and kids all sick, a telephone [which we did not have until required by medical school for emergency calls], all our presents from Sears Christmas catalogue (one of the best Christmases of all), the rare thrill (for both kids and their parents) to go to a Scotts Drive-in movie with popcorn and Kool-aid treats prepared at home to enjoy at the movie, the look of joy on Elisabeth's face when she returned after a week's trip with the kids to St. Louis in the summer to find a new Norge automatic washer installed and working (no more wringer washes for a year. *Consumers' Guide* picked it best buy, but it crashed after one year and was set out on the curb for trash pick up).

INTERNSHIP

As we left St. Louis heading west in early July 1961, I realized that an air-conditioner in the car would have been very nice. I had everything I could possibly get on the top of the station wagon covered with a tarp, but we were still quite crowded. We traveled across Kansas, which seemed rather hot to me. When we stopped for gas, I asked the attendant what the temperature might be, and he said, "I don't know now, but the last time I looked, it was 107." It was, indeed, hot. We stayed at a motel near the Kansas-Colorado state line. There was a rain shower that night which cooled things off. This, together with the increasing elevation, caused the second day to be much cooler. The night before, as we stopped at the motel, I had thought I had *grit* on my face. It was actually crystallized salt from evaporation of perspiration.

As we pulled into sight of the Rockies, I was taken with the inspiring, beautiful view. Fitzsimons General Hospital is in Aurora, Colorado, an eastern suburb of Denver. The hospital loomed large on our right. Seeing this, my stomach churned a bit with apprehension, and then I remembered words of a letter I had received from Bob Taylor, MD, also a graduate of Emory, an Army Reserve buddy, who said, "You will look good here. You know what to do, how to take over in an emergency. These interns from up-east schools haven't had the experience we've had." He was right. His words took on full significance when during the first week of internship, there was an airline crash at Denver's Stapleton International Airport. Although I was not on a rotation that was involved in the care of these patients, this verified Bob's assessment of what I was to face.

We settled into Wherry Housing, which had ample family room in a furnished apartment with an upstairs. We took some of the treasures that had made the long trip by moving van to the dumpster after dark, so they wouldn't be seen. We pared our belongings quite a bit in this way, but I don't guess the darkness really helped, as these same treasures had been unloaded from the moving van in broad daylight.

All in all, we had a delightful year with time to do things on the weekends, as hospital schedule allowed. We spent considerable time in the Falcon seeing the sights and soaking up time together as a family. Bob Taylor's wife, Virginia (Bob was now a surgical resident) told us about a hamburger place not too far from the hospital. The first McDonalds, with which I was to become acquainted, had fast service, with burgers costing a mere sixteen cents. They were quite OK. I was never much of a financial planner. Had I deferred paying of my student loan of $500 and instead, bought McDonalds' stock, I would have had a nice financial nugget. Instead, however, I did pay off my loan within the year and then began whittling away at the Falcon loan.

Incidentally, as time passed, and loans became freely available, many later interns graduated with huge debts incurred, and then increased their indebtedness further during residency, and in essence, lived well, indeed, for those years, unlike the families of interns and residents of my era. When they finally entered practice, their debts were pressing, and they often had a hard-nosed approach to charges assessed their patients. I believe this to be a major factor in the outrageous fees currently charged by some physicians.

From that eventful year in Denver, I can recall several incidents, which are representative of my love of a good story and remember fondly, the following adventures.

A Moving Thank You!

When working the emergency room in Denver, I received a call from an ambulance en route stating that they were bringing in a patient severely beaten in a fight who might arrive DOA. I was waiting at the ER door when he arrived, markedly cyanotic with very limited air exchange, semi-conscious, with bloody, badly beaten face. This being before the AIDS era, I didn't take time to glove up, but plunged my hand into his mouth, pulling out multiple pieces of shattered false teeth, extensive blood clots, and revealing a severely lacerated tongue. His airway restored, I asked, "Is this better?" Not being able to speak, he rolled his head from side to side, tried to smile, and slapped his thighs in affirmation.

He recovered completely, and I hope, learned to duck the next tire tool coming his way.

Cocky Intern

As I was working the same ER, a fellow came in with a dislocated knee. He'd had just enough to drink to be disagreeable and seeing me, he, in bellicose voice, stated, "I want a real doctor, not a damn intern!"

I said, "What you see is what you get. Turn over!" He did and I, never having handled, or much less seen this problem handled, set sail. To my, as well as his amazement, his knee returned to proper alignment. He said something to the effect about my ability being slick or quick or whatever and asked me where I had gone to medical school. I couldn't resist getting even with his initial rudeness, and replied that I'd never been to medical school, but had one day bought a box of Crackerjacks, and the enclosed prize was a medical diploma, and I'd been practicing ever since.

He walked, note, I said *walked* out, dumbfounded.

Foot-in-mouth Disease

When I interned at Fitzsimons General Hospital, senior medical students from the University of Colorado were allowed to take medical or surgical electives there. I remember discussing various aspects of medicine at great lengths with some of these students. During one such session, the student and I were considering the various diseases that we had seen, and our probable reaction should we have these disorders. I said something to the effect, that I had least rather have diabetes than any other common disorder, considering its progressive nature, invading many body systems, and organs and the difficulties of maintaining control. We continued our discussion for several more minutes until he looked at his watch, and said, "Excuse me, time for my insulin shot."

Was Her Name Sarah?

This same student and I, while rotating through OB-GYN, had been up all night with several deliveries, and the next afternoon at weekly conference, it was very difficult to stay awake. He had drifted off, and I was close to doing so when a ninety-three year old lady with vaginal bleeding was presented. The chief of service called on this student to give the single most likely diagnosis. Apparently, he (the student) had heard the vaginal bleeding part of the question, certainly not the ninety-three old part. When his answer was "ectopic (tubal) pregnancy," everyone was wide-awake, if not from the answer, then from the raucous laughter ensuing.

Her name wasn't Sarah, and her husband wasn't Abraham.

First Things First

Interns at Fitzsimons General Hospital rode the ambulance to the scenes of medical need. We took care of active duty Army and Air Force personnel and their dependents as well as retired military personnel, living in the area. One night when I had the duty, a call came in that I fielded. Briefly, this young husband, an enlisted man in the Army, was calling requesting an ambulance to transport his wife to the hospital emergency room. He was in a state of panic, as it was readily learned that his wife was about three months pregnant and was apparently having a miscarriage. When I determined that he lived only two or three blocks off post and explained to him that it would take a few minutes to dispatch the ambulance and considering his strong desire that he needed help "right now," that he could get her to us more quickly than we could get there and back. I suggested that he place towels in the front seat, pick her up, and place her in the car, and be on his way to the ER. He rebelled at this, asking, "And get blood all over my car?"

EARLY BIRD GETS THE WORM
ERRR EXAM

This did not happen to me but did happen to a fellow intern at Fitzsimons Hospital. He had just gotten to sleep about four a.m. on a Sunday morning after a long night of taking care of patients in the emergency room when the nurse awakened him. She said, "There are four children of one family to see you."

The intern asked, "What – a car wreck?"

The nurse replied, "No, they had started to the mountains for a Sunday outing and remembered that the kids had not yet had their pre-school physicals." It was not reported to me what the doctor said.

GUT FEELING

Another memorable experience of the ER, concerned an early evening phone call from the wife of a retired Army sergeant. She related that when her husband took out the garbage (even military men take out the garbage – a male duty), he came back with a before, unnoticed, grayish pallor of his face, and some pain in his chin and neck. Not liking the sound of this, I said we'd be right out. The patient/husband was good naturedly miffed at his wife for calling and apologized to us for the trouble. He now had no pain, and his facial color was normal. Physical examination with a special emphasis on his cardiovascular system was without significant findings. I told him my findings, and then asked the ambulance personnel to bring in the litter.

He really squawked at this, and I confabulated a bit saying, "It is my policy if I come out to see you, you go home (ER) with me." Truth is I had a strange, powerful gut feeling about this patient, and it was not good. He got on the litter, refusing aid in so doing. We started down the hall of his modest home and "whatta ya know," the litter was too long to negotiate the corner in his hallway. So off the litter, he walked to the door, and back onto the litter. I joked with him about this saying, "If President Eisenhower could walk into Fitzsimons Hospital with a heart attack, you can too." We both then laughed, and as we started toward the hospital, he supported himself on one elbow saying, "If you're going to take me to the hospital, let me show you the closest way."

We followed his directions, arrived at the hospital, and even before I got his workup for MI underway, the medical officer of the day was on my case, "Why did you bring this guy in? He's not sick." He outranked me, but I convinced him that since the patient was there, that we should, at least, do the tests. He grudgingly acceded. The tests were all negative. Now, that officer wanted him sent home. I put on a Grammy or Academy Award performance, pleading my case, but I really was not acting as I was convinced totally, and without reservation that the patient was a cardiac time bomb, so he was admitted, reevaluated periodically through the night, and early the next morning about the time I was having breakfast, had a massive coronary. If you have to have one of those, it is better done in a hospital setting. All the right ingredients were in place for managing such a medical catastrophe; thus, he was treated by the cardiologist, responded well, and survived. In a few days, he sent for me and was effusive in his thanks. Upon his discharge, which was two weeks, minimum in those days, he said in the presence of his gathered family that I was the doctor who had said that he was going to have his heart attack before he had it. 'Tain't so. 'Twas gut reaction. [Nothing feels so good as to help someone in a meaningful way when no one else can or no one else will.]

During these Denver days, Bob Taylor and I were able to get away for a weekend of deer hunting and did well, bringing in three deer. We enjoyed family picnics and excursions and a most memorable Memorial Day, spent camping on the Platte River. Army medical life was good enough, the medical training excellent, and wearing a uniform became second nature. All in all, my tenure at Denver as an intern was pleasant both from the standpoint of work and leisure.

With the influence of John Reisner, the Chief of Dermatology at Fitzsimons General Hospital, I received an Army residency in dermatology.

DERMATOLOGY RESIDENCY

After completion of internship in Denver, I entered a dermatology residency at Brooke Army Medical Center in San Antonio, Texas.

I like Texas and Texans and find them outgoing and friendly people. Some say they are nice partially because the harshness of the climate causes them to seek refuge in their friends. Maybe.

General Sheridan is supposed to have said, "If I owned Hell and owned Texas, I should choose to live in Hell and rent out Texas."

The first year of my residency there, the temperature reached a hundred degrees in April. The kids went barefoot on Christmas Day, and we had twenty plus consecutive days of one hundred degrees or higher, and I think well over a month without measurable rain. When it did rain, we were eating supper, and just like in the movies, when rain finally came breaking the drought, we all left the table, went out, and stood there getting wet, enjoying the feeling.

I like audacity in measured doses and pride exhibited by Texans. When I first went to San Antonio, the main post office had but four letter drop slots – number one, **Texas**; number two, **Local**; number three, **Airmail and Special Delivery**; number four, **Other States and Foreign**. Some years ago, I went back to check this out. The labels are now politically correct and bland.

Sometime during my three years there, a Northwestern Mutual Insurance Agent, (B. P.) enticed me into buying some life insurance from him. During the conversation after he had learned that my medical degree came from Emory, he asked if I knew Uncle Bud. The answer was "No, at least, not by that name," and he seemed surprised. Then when he furnished the last name, I promptly recognized this prominent member of the faculty and the chief of his branch of specialization who was well known to all medical students. He was, perhaps, the most disliked of the entire faculty.

As the story goes, this physician/faculty member had done a surgical procedure at the Federal Correctional Institute in Atlanta where he had been assigned a prisoner scrub nurse. As this surgeon was known to do, he threw the surgical sponges on the opposite side to where the bucket was located. Whenever the bucket was moved to the other side, he threw the sponges to where the bucket had been, all the while complaining effusively of the incompetence of the help.

Soon tiring of this, the prisoner/nurse said to the surgeon, "Look Bud, I'm doing life for murder, the worst sentence there is. If you don't throw the *blankety, blank* sponges in the bucket, they're going to have me with a new charge for the same offense."

So according to the story "Uncle Bud" adapted promptly (and quietly) to the "request."

Is this not a widely traveled reputation going from Georgia to Texas?

My years at Brooke, 1962 – 1965 were filled with incidents and people that have remained favorites over the years. Following are some of those precious memories:

"DR." FELIX
MEETING MR. DERMATOLOGY SERVICE

After I reported to Brooke Army Medical Center, I drove down to the dermatology section of the hospital and met Felix

*John, David, and Ann during Dermatology residency days,
circa 1962, San Antonio, Texas*

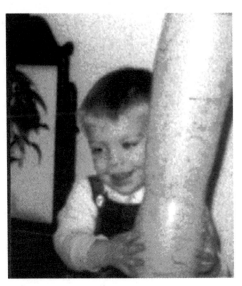

*Franky, our youngest child. Photo taken at
Fort Knox, circa 1966*

Sandlin, the clerk, an actual power behind the throne, much like a Master Sergeant in the combat arms branches of the Army. One of the first questions he asked was what was my religion. When I said, "Baptist," he said, "Another damned Baptist!" Owen Wister was right when he penned in *The Virginian*, "When you say that, smile!" He smiled and we became life-long friends.

I spent several minutes chatting with him, and while there, Colonel George Prazac, the Chief of Dermatology, checked in with Felix, and we were introduced. Colonel Prazac asked what I was doing and my response was, "Walk-in clinic pending beginning residency training."

The Colonel, in addition to his dermatology duties, was acting Deputy Commander of Brooke Army Medical Center, and in that role, he told me to come down and start work at the Dermatology Clinic the next morning, that he would take care of the paper work. He was an impressive looking officer. He had jet-black hair, was slim for his age, and was forceful in his demeanor. His retirement was eminent, and I could not help thinking that he'd make a fine general. He is now well into his eighties with health problems, but I call him about every three months to check on him. When I first called him, after some years' gap in our relationship, I asked if he remembered me. He said, "Yes, you are one of the few to thank me for their residency training." He is a true friend, having rendered a big favor without being asked.

The residency went well from the start. Felix was one of the old-time Venereology specialists and could tell me much that was not in the books on this subject. He had experience in many areas of therapy (considered barbaric by today's standards) for this group of diseases. Colonel Darl Vander Ploeg was the next Chief and sort of over-mothered us as we began our residency, but then he was feeling his way also since he had not headed a residency-training program before.

My brother Leon and his wife Ruth lived in Ft. Worth, and we visited back and forth once or twice yearly. In the spring of

1965, I answered a phone call in the wee hours from my oldest brother's (Ralph) doctor informing me that my brother's wife had killed him in a domestic argument. I left later that morning for Biloxi, Mississippi and made funeral arrangements for him. This brought to mind another tragedy when in 1948, his first wife died leaving two children, a girl, Martha Elizabeth, almost seven years old, and a son, Frank, eight months old from that marriage. The children's aunt assumed responsibility for Martha and my mother and father reared Frank.

THE SHINING LIGHT

Felix Sandlin was one of the smartest people that I have ever known. While he did have business training, he had no professional medical training. However, his intellect had no bounds in any endeavor he chose to pursue, especially in the areas of medicine and mechanics. Combining these two fields, he invented and held patents on three inventions, and most

Glenn with Faye and Felix Sandlin, close friends
from San Antonio, Texas, circa 1995

notably invented a cryosurgical unit used by many dermatologists and other physicians in many states.

I had been at Brooke but a short time when the incandescent bulb that we used as a source of light for one of our microscopes burned out. I asked Felix for a replacement.

He said, "Let's see if we can fix that one."

Fix a light bulb? Unbelievable!

He took the light bulb, inspected it very carefully, screwed the bulb back into the lamp, positioned it, and plugged it in. The bulb functioned again, and lasted several months longer. I think the secret is to tilt the bulb so that the filament comes very close to the residual burned-out segment, and sometimes the electricity will cause an arc to bridge the small gap causing the bulb to be functional.

Happily, for light bulb manufacturers, it doesn't work every time.

THE CUSSIN'

Felix had an intuitive mind and could get to the bottom of the problem in a hurry. He understood mechanical things and was a born tinkerer. If he couldn't get it going, junk it. The Assistant Chief of Dermatology had bought a new lawn mower and could not get it started no matter how hard he tried. In desperation, he asked Felix to come over on a Saturday morning and see what he could do. When Felix arrived, he saw, at a glance, the problem. Now, this dermatologist was very religious. Never would he use a questionable word or phrase. Of course, Felix knew this and incorporated this knowledge into his performance.

He launched into a considerable discourse holding that on occasion even mechanical things had to be corrected, had to be coerced into a functional state and deduced "a good cussin' would do the trick." He launched into the pedigree and every aspect of the new lawn mower. At some point during this verbal assault when the owner's head was turned away, Felix was able to turn the fuel switch to the "On" position from" OFF" without being noticed. He finished his cussin' by saying, "That ought to be enough," pulled the recoil starter, and it started with the first pull.

Felix was not one to tell his tricks; thus, he never revealed the cause of the problem to the owner of the balky lawn mower.

Judy and I had some wonderful trips to San Antonio to visit with Felix and his dear wife, Faye during which Felix and I had opportunity to reminisce about those bygone days. I treasure the memory of these visits as well.

Felix has been dead now about five years and I truly miss him.

"Oops" Not Spoken Here

As a dermatology resident, I felt that some training and experience in minor surgery would be helpful, so I did a rotation in plastic surgery.

One day during surgery as I was doing a procedure, I fumbled a bit at what I was doing and innocently said, "Oops!"

The real surgeon supervising me temporarily stopped the procedure and gave me a complete lecture with the subject being "Oops is a word that we *do not* use in surgery!"

Little Things Mean a Lot — Bugged

In 1963 or 1964, I attended the Texas State Muzzleloading Rifle shoot in San Angelo, with B. A. Campbell, a spry seventy-something year old. There we competed in the Civil War Musket category, firing at bull's eye targets at fifty yards. He was shooting an original Enfield musket, and the best score possible per shot was ten points and the least score a five, or a zero, if a miss. He fired, getting an eight on his first shot, and as all firing was muzzleloading with the powder being measured, he noted a last year's June bug in his powder measure. He shook it out on the ground, measured the powder, and fired his second shot – a six. He then measured his powder again and fired – a five. I was concentrating on my own shooting, but when I looked over his way, here was this elderly man crawling around on the ground sifting through the accumulated debris.

"B. A., what are you looking for?"

His answer, "My damn bug."

Not Fox, Wolf, Swan, or Crow – It's Chicken

I was watering the lawn when I lived in San Antonio, and I'll tell you now that if one has a lawn in San Antonio, he will spend a heap of time and money watering to bring this to pass. I noticed a moving van pulling away across the street, so I went over to meet my new neighbor. I introduced myself and learned that his name was Dan Chicken. I suppressed a smile, but sometime later, when I also learned his wife's maiden name, I could just hear the minister who officiated at their wedding saying, "Do you, Daniel Chicken, take Paula Pennypecker to be . . . .."

How funny!

Small World # 1

Master Sergeant Okla W. Thornton was my First Sergeant in Korea and I was very fond of him. I left Korea in 1953, and then attended graduate school, then medical school, and when I was in dermatology residency in Texas 1962 – 1965 and walked into an examining room to see the next patient, there was my old friend, Oke." Oh, happy reunion!

DERMATOLOGIST

IRELAND ARMY HOSPITAL

On April 16, 1965, a son Frank Stephen was born, and in August we moved to Fort Knox, Kentucky, where I had been assigned to Ireland Army Hospital. I had passed through Kentucky a number of times over the years and had greatly admired that beautiful state and liked the people based on my brief encounters. We then lived on base in government housing, and after settling in, I began preliminary preparation for the written part of Dermatology Board Certification to be given in about nine months in St. Louis. I met a retired Army Colonel, James M. VanDivier, who was very much into making and shooting Kentucky Flintlock Longrifles. I had long been interested in old-time muzzleloading rifles and had done well, but a flintlock was a new challenge. Under his tutelage and with use of his shop on my afternoon off, I crafted one that shot well enough to place me on the Kentucky Longrifle Team after becoming a member of the Corps of Kentucky Longriflemen. Over the years, our team competed with Pennsylvania, Tennessee, Indiana, Georgia, and I believe, Ohio.

Since I had signed an agreement to repay the Army with three years service for the three-year Dermatology Residency I had received, I expected to be separated from the Army about the first of August 1968. However, the Surgeon General pulled a fast one, freezing those of us who were affected and delaying

Kentucky Longrifle Team taken at Daniel Boone Festival, Barbourville, Kentucky, circa 1968: (L to R) Front row: Don Wells (deceased), Norton Gatz, Col. James VanDivier (deceased), Ronnie Fuller, Bob Filson Row 2: Al Leaf, John Hockersmith, Waldo Lacy, Harold Ellington, Taylor Ellington (deceased), John Meisenheimer, Glenn Marsh. Photo courtesy of John Hockersmith

our separation for a proposed one year. Feeling, this to be illegal, I put up strong opposition. There were spelled out reasons which could be used to extend an officer's commitment, but none of these conditions were met, and after a tense standoff, I was separated after eleven extra days of duty that did not unduly affect my plans to open my practice in Lexington, Kentucky, the Tuesday after Labor Day, 1968.

During my tenure at Fort Knox, Dr. Winston U. Rutledge from Louisville was the dermatology consultant and while old enough to be my father, treated me like a brother. He was one of the finest individuals I've ever known. Coming from Virginia, he still retained a bit of the old Dominion in his speech and bearing. He was a true Southern gentleman. My family, as well

Dr. Winston U. Rutledge receiving a commendation from Colonel Williams, Hospital Commander of Ireland Army Hospital, Fort Knox, Kentucky. Glenn, Chief of Dermatology at Ireland, nominated Dr. Rutledge for this award.

as I, loved him. Mainly because of Dr. Rutledge, I looked forward to the Kentucky Medical Association meeting held in Louisville each September when he and I would have lunch and attend the dermatology session in the afternoon. That evening, members of the Kentucky Dermatologic Society with their wives would have dinner at the Pendennis Club, all arranged by Dr. Rutledge. We would go by, Elisabeth and I, to see Mrs. Rutledge before dinner as she was in poor health and unable to attend the social function. She was as gracious and charming as he. Sadly, both are now deceased.

Dr. Rutledge set aside one-half to one full day a week for reading professional literature. This self-discipline made for a good, well-informed, up-to-date consultant. I found his studious nature an inspiration for my own medical career, and I have, even through my retirement, continued, as did he, to read my professional journals.

Many of the stories and incidents involving this wonderful colleague as well as those days at Fort Knox are undoubtedly lost to memory, but following are two of those that remain indelible in current memory:

DR. RUTLEDGE AND HIS PET PEEVE

His pet peeve was to be accosted in public and addressed something as follows – "Hi, Dr. Rutledge, I'll bet you don't remember me."

His stock answer went something like this, "Of course, I do. I saw you sometime ago with syphilis. How are you doing?"

DR. RUTLEDGE
GENETICS VS. DISEASE

Dr. Rutledge had but a fringe of hair above ear level, but was totally bald upward of this point. Hair growth from this level downward was normal.

Once a father brought his son to see Dr. Rutledge because of hair loss. When Dr. Rutledge entered the room, the son said to his father, not discretely, after noting Dr. Rutledge's bald pate, "I think we've got the wrong doctor."

Dr. Rutledge heard this, then having noted the moth-eaten characteristics of the young man's hair loss, and thus, having already made the correct diagnosis said curtly, "Young man, my hair loss is because of genetics – yours is because of syphilis."

The young man was treated properly for syphilis, regrew his hair, but alas, Dr. Rutledge was stuck with his baldness because of unfavorable genes.

CLINIC DIRECTIONS

I have always been impressed with the American G.I.'s ingenuity. At Ireland Army Hospital at Fort Knox, Kentucky, both the orthopedic brace shop and the chaplain's office were located across the hall from each other in the basement. Some enterprising G.I. made a sign similar to the following drawing:

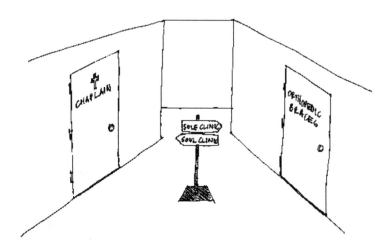

PRIVATE PRACTICE

The Marsh family moved from Fort Knox to Lexington, Kentucky in August, 1968. My office would be 117 West Second Street, in an older home converted to an office, actually two medical offices. An internist rented the upstairs and the downstairs was my dermatology office. It was small but adequate, as I needed no space for storage of medical records, yet. Dr. C.C. Barrett, a dermatologist, owned and had occupied the office for a number of years. I had met him at the annual meeting of the Kentucky Dermatologic Society held in conjunction with the Kentucky Medical Society when I first came to Kentucky and saw him at least once a year thereafter.

Slightly over a year before I completed my requisite pay back time to the Army for my dermatology training, he was attending an international dermatology meeting in Germany and became quite ill. He never fully recovered and after an unsuccessful attempt to return to practice, he retired. I do not recall how I learned of the availability of his office, but I pursued the matter and reached an agreement for the use of his office and his equipment. He did not have late model equipment, except his x-ray machine, but he certainly practiced correct and up-to-date dermatology. I had not known him very well, but we became better acquainted, and I developed a genuine liking, actually affection and respect, for this gentleman and physician.

On Tuesday following Labor Day 1968, the office opened with Elisabeth as secretary and Glenn as dermatologist. We had not developed sufficient office routine, and when the last patient departed, it was quite late, consequently, the baby-sitter for our youngest was angry, but we were on our way. The next day, I think I saw but three or four patients; nevertheless, we had made a start.

Dr. C. C. Barrett

When I took over Dr. Barrett's office, I found notes and directions concerning the oldest/largest specimens of the various kinds of trees indigenous to Kentucky, this being of particular interest to him. He did not schedule patients but was simply at his office during usual office hours and was thus available. The office was close to the downtown bus station, and several patients from Eastern Kentucky used this mode of transportation to come see him. Parking was limited to two or three spaces and the building next-door was the office of a psychiatrist, who seemed to hold me personally responsible if one of my patients parked in one of his reserved spaces. I never did convince him that I was not a part of a plot to occupy his reserved spaces.

Since Dr. Barrett did not make appointments and was not a "come back" dermatologist, enough patients, who did not know that Dr. Barrett had retired, drifted in to sustain me while I built my own practice.

Dr. Barrett was a most considerate physician, and I learned a lot about him from what his former patients told me as well as from his patient charts. He was conservative in patient management and ultra-conservative in his charges and in his patients' records.

The office situated downtown as it was, allowed a short walk to the "Y" for a wholesome, inexpensive lunch. This is the historic Gratz Park area and was particularly beautiful when fall came with the attendant colors. Transylvania University was only one long block away, and the original site of the Lexington Clinic was directly across the street. A pharmacy was at the nearest corner, and several physicians still had offices in this area. All in all, this was a less expensive way to get started.

The following illustrates Dr. Barrett's concise, to the point, don't mince words approach.

To The Point

One day an extremely agitated, deranged, delusional, old lady, a former patient of Dr. Barrett's, came in. She insisted that some men had held her down and branded her nose with their initials. She demanded that I look at the nonexistent scars.

Having learned by this time of Dr. Barrett's concise language in assessing patient information, I anxiously looked up her record. His clinical entry was five words, "A crazy, psychotic old woman." He saw her six months later and had reduced his clinical record to two words, "Still crazy!"

No charges were assessed for visits with him or me.

He also could be misunderstood by those who misread his personality as I had originally, thinking him standoffish and somewhat pompous. How wrong I was!

A Gauntlet Thrown Down

When I was asked to see, on consultation, my first hospital patient at the Offutt Pavilion of Good Samaritan Hospital (this building now long replaced) I met Dr. Nicholas Kavanaugh, an internist. After I introduced myself, he told me very bluntly that he hoped I would not be like most of the other dermatologists in the city – see the patient, have multiple, he inferred unnecessary, visits and finally return the patient to the referring doctor only after the patient was broke. Welcome to Medical Economics 101. Feeling that a gauntlet had been flung down at my feet, I was stunned, almost angered by his brusque manner.

In a conciliatory manner, that is supposed to and did turn away wrath, I told him that was not my way at all, never had been, and a trial referral or two was in order. He did refer a few patients initially, and as the years passed, referred preferentially to me and was apparently quite pleased. I also learned something of him. He was brilliant at clinical-pathological conferences wherein a difficult-to-diagnose patient was presented, complete with history, physical examination, and laboratory results. He, above all others, would usually suggest the correct diagnosis. He was also harder on himself than others. While not very popular with patients who did not follow his directions or with what he considered less than dedicated fellow practitioners, he was forthright, dedicated, and single minded. Though he was a somewhat difficult man, I liked him, respected him, and referred rheumatology patients to him, but only those who were very serious about their illness and would be likely to follow his directions. Those patients respected him, did well, and liked him.

BEDSIDE MANNER VS. ABILITY

Early one morning, before 7:00 a.m., I was seated, reviewing charts, out of sight of the hospital elevator and nurses' station, and hidden from view by a divider which held charts, but scarcely obstructed my view.

The elevator opened and a G.P. whom I knew well, stepped out and greeted the nurses with, "My, my you ladies are all so beautiful. I'm glad I don't have to decide which is the loveliest. How are all of you today?" This is not all of the conversation, but enough to reveal his manner (blarney). His conversation continued and finally, he turned down the hall where he had patients. The nurses were all a twitter, "He is the nicest man! He is such a good doctor, wonderful person." I knew differently and took silent exception to his line and the nurses' evaluation of his competence.

A moment or two later, the elevator again opened and off stepped Nick Kavanaugh. The nurses still basking in Dr. "Blarney's" fawning said, "Good morning, Dr. Kavanaugh, how are you?"

He replied, "Fine, get me the nursing supervisor!"

"Is there something wrong?" one asked.

"Yes, get me the nursing supervisor," said this time with a tone of "do it NOW."

The supervisor was there within three or four minutes and Dr. Kavanaugh went right to the point. He addressed her by name, then said, "I was here with – the patient's name – upon admission last evening. I ordered such and such medicine to be given 'stat' and she did not receive it for at least forty-five minutes. At the price patients pay to be in this hospital, they deserve better attention and service than that!"

The nurse without defense simply said, "Yes, Sir."

Nick turned down the same hallway as Dr. "Blarney," and the nurses' comments were revealing, "He's a terrible man and terrible doctor. I'd never go to see him."

These comments fit the first doctor, not Nick Kavanaugh. He was guilty of wanting the very best for his patients.

Supporting Cast
Dennis Penn, MD

If forced to name the one physician who helped me most in my earliest days of practice, other than Jim Bard, it would certainly be Dr. Dennis Penn, a pediatrician, immensely popular with young parents and very talented in his specialty. I cannot ever recall hearing a complaint from any patient or parent about him.

After almost a year downtown and seeing the trend of medical offices moving to the southern part of the city, I decided that downtown was a dying medical area. Subsequent events proved this to be correct. I had tentatively decided on an empty office in Medical Plaza on Nicholasville Road. I asked Dr. Penn's advice and he suggested Medical Heights at 2368 Nicholasville Road. There was one suite remaining for lease, Suite 301, with outside windows, just what the dermatologist ordered. I signed on in this brand-new building where I spent twenty memorable years. In one of life's real ironies, just after my retirement, Dr. Penn occupied my former office the two years prior to his retiring from medical practice. Subsequently, he became Fayette County coroner. Thank you again, Dennis and Brenda.

Chase Allen, MD

Chase Allen, a plastic surgeon upstairs on the same end of the building as I, was an absolutely marvelous person with whom to work. I believe I shared more success in patient management and true service rendered in conjunction with this kind, even-tempered physician than with any other practitioner. What a great guy with whom to work! He preceded me by a few years into retirement, and I don't believe I know anyone who enjoyed this aspect of his life more. I know his philosophy of medical practice was quite similar to mine.

Jim Butler, MD John Garden, MD; Walt Brewer, MD

Another highly respected fellow practitioner, Dr. Jim Butler, was already in practice when I came to town. He also graciously welcomed me and kindly referred to me as I did to him.

Dr. John Garden, an ophthalmologist, and Dr. Walt Brewer, a urologist, established their practices about the same time as I, and they have remained cherished friends and confidants over the years rendering excellent care for my family and me.

These outstanding physicians whom I have mentioned as being so very supportive and dedicated to the medical profession are, indeed, the best – the "gold" – in "The Golden Age of Medicine."

Office Memories

Many memorable experiences occurred during my time in this office location including a fire originating in or near the psychiatrist's office upstairs, many quick lunches in the nearby restaurants, multiple new and lasting friendships formed, jokes played on the staff, and jokes played on the doctor by the staff.

Teaching Approach

When I, as resident in dermatology, was given the duty of teaching interns, I resolved to learn from what I believed to be gross error in the teaching philosophy to which I was subjected during my time at Emory. Thus, I, over time, developed my teaching approach and once after giving a lecture to the sophomore, perhaps, junior medical students, I received a standing ovation. That made all the preparation worthwhile and brought vast satisfaction.

I had been in practice only a few months when I started donating some of my time for teaching at the University of Kentucky College of Medicine both through lecturing and conducting clinics. Toward the latter part of my practice, I no longer did lectures or clinics at the University, but the Family Practice Department required their residents to rotate through my office for their dermatology training. They taught me medicine, I taught them dermatology, and I made many fine friends through this relationship.

One of these is now a United States Congressman and one, Dr. Richie Van Bussum, my family physician. I see in him kindness, caring, interest, dedication, and ability that in days past one would have routinely expected to have received from his/her physician. It is a tonic for my soul to witness his integrity and enthusiasm for the noble profession of medicine.

Kind words from my former students would, on occasion, filter back to me by way of mutual acquaintances in which they, referring to me, said something to the effect: "He taught me what dermatology I know, but more importantly he taught me the great principles of medicine and life." I considered that the supreme accolade, but, of course, this principle of life came from the greatest Teacher of all who said, "Do unto others as you would have them do unto you."

THE THREE A'S

Prior to opening my office in Lexington, I made an appointment with Dr. Irving Kanner, now deceased, an established internist, in order to get his suggestions relative to the practice of medicine in Lexington.

He suggested as a guide, the three A's – Able, Available, and Affable. Reviewing my credentials, he felt me to be able and made a few comments on being promptly available, and then stressed the importance of being of an agreeable nature, i.e. affable. Soon after the opening of my office, I was requested by another physician to see a patient in the hospital. Now, I did know that I was Able, and goodness knows in those slow early days, I was certainly Available, so when calling upon the patient, I suppose Affable was definitely on the agenda.

Somewhat breezily I swept into the room of this old geezer, his age then, about my age now, and flashing my best Pepsodent smile said too loudly, "Hi, I'm Glenn Marsh. I'm in the skin (dermatology) game!"

He visibly recoiled and remarked defensively and crossly, "Aren't all of you?" Well, actually he was in the *skin game* since he never paid me.

GENERAL OFFICE PROCEDURE AND ATTITUDES

I learned early that courteous, knowledgeable, considerate, and kind employees with excellent telephone manners were a must. As a telephone call is usually the first contact one has with the office, an opinion is thus formed, and it should be a good one. I stressed this as well as personal greetings being given when any patient came to the office. We had but one rule in personal relationships, which was to treat everyone the way you'd want to be treated.

We had a few patient complaints a year about the bill; other than errors in bookkeeping. I'd listen to the complaint without interruption, and if further explanation were needed, I was happy to comply. If the complaint were related to the amount of the bill only, my usual response was to state clearly that it was my policy never to argue about anything, especially a bill and that if the patient were dissatisfied with the charge, the patient should pay what he/she felt appropriate, including the option to pay nothing. This worked exceptionally well. Over the years, I saw several patients whom I felt were unable to pay, but because of their personal pride, I felt that not charging them would be a disservice because they would not have returned out of this pride, not wishing to be a burden. For these dear, sensitive patients, I would assess a token charge, a dollar or two. This approach also worked well.

When I told my patients of my decision to retire, some of these dependent patients broke into tears; a few felt abandoned, but I also told them that they would be cared for by Dr. James Bard at the Lexington Clinic with whom I had had a very close professional relationship over the years and for whom I held the deepest respect. Their fears were unrealized as Dr. Bard, not only maintained care for these folks at little or no charge, but come Christmas, did me one better. His office staff agreed to forego the usual in-office exchange of presents and instead had a Christmas party for L. J. one of my most destitute former patients, giving to her these presents. This is proof that caring is present in many health care professionals.

Over the years, while loving my profession, in general, and my specialty, in particular, I developed an especial fondness not only for youngsters, especially teenagers, but also for older folks. My favorite "smile bringer" was to ask, at the end of the office visit, an elderly patient who had been a loyal patient over the years, "When is your birthday?" Of course, having his/her medical chart in hand, I already knew. If his/her birthday had already passed or was upcoming, the "pitch" was modified to fit and went something like this, "Everybody deserves a freebie now and then and today is your day! Today's visit is your [early/late, to fit the situation] birthday present."

I overdid this on one occasion and my secretary said, "Dr. Marsh, it's 10:30 (I started at 8:00 a.m.) and you haven't charged a single patient yet."

I replied, "Yes, but I'm having fun." One old fellow, about my current age, was so elated, he told everyone in his community and the word got back to me, allowing me to share his happiness twice.

KINDNESS RETURNED

Some armchair philosophers feel that a kindness rendered is one that will someday return to the "giver." I am a proponent of this philosophy and believe that the following is evidence of the validity of this belief.

The incident to which I refer occurred in Berea, Kentucky. My wife Judy traveling alone bumped bumpers, but with damage occurring to neither car. The young driver of the other car was bellicose, offensive, and somewhat harassing. Judy called the police and an officer responded. He asked to see the drivers' license of both drivers, separately, of course, and when he saw the name Judy Marsh, with a Lexington address, asked if she were related to Dr. Marsh in Lexington. Upon telling him that I was her husband, he told Judy that he always took his elderly father to his appointment with me, and how gracious and considerate I had been to his father and other elderly patients. He then examined both cars and finding neither damaged, he sent the bent-out-of-shape young man home with some strong fatherly advice.

NO SMOKING

Ours was one of the first offices to prohibit smoking in the waiting room. My cigar smoker patient came in, stogie in mouth, and when Barbara told him most respectfully that smoking wasn't permitted in the waiting room, he ground out his lighted cigar on a leather covered table burning a hole. The new hole was adjacent to the ashtray placed there for extinguishing smoking materials.

Some people!

The Old Farmer and His Wife

My patient census included a large number of country people, which suited me fine, as I fit that category.

One day a large raw-boned farmer accompanied by his wife came into the examining room. After I introduced myself, he got right to the point saying, "Doc, I want you to fix my *womern*. I wouldn't take a million dollars *fur* her, but on the other hand, I wouldn't give a dime for *anuthern*."

Misunderstanding *Alabamese*

When I'd get behind in seeing patients, I would utilize my office as an extra exam room for seeing return patients, not requiring disrobing, for example, "hand eczema." This backfired on one notable occasion. The patient so placed had psoriasis and had evidently rubbed or scratched while awaiting my entrance. When he left, there was a mini-snow fall of psoriatic skin scales surrounding the chair. I told my technician that the room would require cleaning before use with another patient. He asked what the problem was, and I said without enunciating clearly, "The last patient *shed* all over the carpet." I was near the end of the sentence before I realized how much *shed* sounded like another four-letter word especially in *Alabamese*. When I caught the similarity, I only made the matter not worse, but hopelessly worse, by spelling the word. "That's **s-h-e-d**."

Gales of laughter emanated from all the exam rooms from those patients who had heard the exchange and subsequently spread to the waiting room so that all could enjoy my gaffe.

Visual Aid/On Being Very Observant

On another occasion, when my office was again being used as an exam room, the patient who had been sitting there for sometime, removed a reference book from the bookshelf to peruse, and when I came into the room, he said, "I think I've found what's wrong with me."

I said, "Let me examine you and we'll compare notes." After I told him the diagnosis, he showed me a picture in the book and, lo and behold, he was right. I then told him that I reserved the right to prescribe the correct medicine and he exited laughing.

Many patients are very observant; on my extensive bookshelves, there were many volumes with titles covering not only dermatology, but pediatrics, surgery, internal medicine, X-ray, and radium as well. The patient ensconced in my office had noted these, but had spotted the one book not related to medicine entitled *The Rise and Fall of Jesse James* by Robertus Love. "Why this book?" he asked.

I replied that, at one time, I was a serious student of the James family and that this was one of my favorite books on the subject.

MALPRACTICE – ADAM AND EVE

I was never sued for malpractice, but threatened once. The details: an orthopedic surgeon admitted a patient for evaluation for back surgery. Among the admission orders was a request for a dermatology consultation with me.

I saw the patient promptly, diagnosed his psoriasis, and placed him on external medications, one during the day and the other for overnight use with polyethylene wrap occlusion, which made the medicine twenty times more effective.

Two days later, the nurse on his floor called to say that he would not be having surgery after all and was being discharged. She also added that he had a new rash so the nurse was instructed that he not be discharged until I could see him there in the hospital or if he wished, he could be discharged with clear cut instructions to come by my office so that I might see him. I suspected a reaction to his medications, but when he arrived, and was examined, the limit of involvement coincided perfectly with those areas covered by the occlusive wrap. His skin was slightly pink only, with no blisters, and most wonderfully, he had experienced a prompt response to the treatment given, his psoriasis being dramatically improved. Polyethylene is considered inert, and this was the first and only reaction to it I have ever seen. I advised him that the pinkness would disappear in a couple of days or so, but also instructed him to discontinue use of the occlusive wrap.

Two days later, I received a letter advising of an impending malpractice suit. I called my malpractice carrier. The representative of my insurance company came by and coincidentally while he was there in the office discussing the problem, a second letter came from the patient saying that he had changed his mind and would not sue. By this time, I would guess, that his psoriasis had cleared temporarily, and also his polyethylene induced pink skin had cleared permanently.

When the patient saw his referring orthopedist again, this doctor asked him why he wanted to sue Dr. Marsh. He said that it was his wife's idea. She was reportedly quoted as saying, "All doctors have lots of money; we may as well get some."

If Wishes Were Horses –

"If wishes were horses, then beggars might ride," was a saying that my mother would use frequently. As I recall, there was also usually a following corollary I would hear from her after my saying, "I wish, I wish . . . ." This follow-up phrase was something to the effect, "Don't just wish; work to make it come about, and it will."

However, we all have fantasies for which we wish. I often noted these wishes by some of my patients during my practice of dermatology; I remember a pleasant lady who came to see me for a hair loss problem consisting of bald patches rather than diffuse thinness. The hair remaining was of a non-descript color and apparently gave her some problems with management and/or styling. I told her that injections into the bald areas would probably cause regrowth, which was likely to be permanent and remain after cessation of the injections. She elected to have this procedure, and in short order, all of the treated areas responded, and to her delight, there was complete regrowth at the time of her last visit – not only regrowth, but also regrowth with jet black, lustrous, naturally curly hair. She was ecstatic and with much hope and anticipation requested that I inject the whole scalp. It was my regretful task to tell her that was not possible and that over time, while her new hair would remain, it would take on the characteristics, color, and texture of the surrounding hair.

"If wishes were horses. . . ."

MEDICAL EMERGENCY

My receptionist made a priority appointment for a black patient. When he came in, he stated his problem succinctly, "My skin was turnin' white and that is a medical emergency!" This reminded me of the reverse situation when years ago, a white lady came in and wanted me to turn her skin black as she had a black boyfriend.

I wasn't of help in either situation.

WHAT TRIBE IS THAT?

During the latter part of my dermatology career, I had a clinic once weekly at the Harrison County Hospital in Cynthiana, Kentucky.

One day a well-dressed male patient came to see me. Actually, he was more than well dressed – in the language of the day, he was a *sharp dresser*. After the usual pleasantries had been exchanged, I asked him how might I be of help to him. He answered, "I have a problem with my *gentiles*."

I suppressed a hint of a smile – I hope not much crossed my countenance. He then quickly recovered saying, "That's not right, my *genteels*."

I liked dermatology as a specialty for a number of reasons including the following: there were no age restrictions, new-born to octogenarian; it included both sexes; and most of all, there were few life-threatening diseases with which to contend, and even fewer life-threatening emergency situations. This allowed a certain amount of levity not enjoyed by other medical specialties, at least, not on a more or less continual basis. Dermatology being a specialty that has few of these situations with grave consequences has, to my knowledge, never been a subject of interest to TV viewers; however, lacking these cliffhangers, we can appeal to the humor that is in us all.

One lady said, though not in a condemning way, "Dr. Marsh, coming to your office is just like watching *MASH* on television."

I said, "Oh, thank you. That is the best compliment we'll get all week."

And so was the case in the office on more than one occasion, especially on April Fool's Day, Halloween, and any other day we could work in an excuse to let our hair down. The fun was innocent, though imaginative, and I don't recall but one or two instances where things went a bit too far, my fault, of course.

SECRETARIES – GOOD AND BAD

During the years the office staff had some parties, and we would not infrequently have lunch at nearby restaurants. There were also a very few going away parties as we mostly had the same staff for years. My two best, and longest tenured, secretaries were both named Barbara and both left my employment moving out of state because of their husbands, one Barbara to marry, the other, a job relocation for her husband. Both were missed greatly, as would be family, and both maintained ties, especially my "Ohio daughter" as Barbara M. is called. She never misses our wedding anniversary, birthdays, Father's Day, holidays, such as Easter and especially Christmas. She has the best memory for names of anyone I have ever met, and she and her family are considered our family. My other Barbara B. lives in Missouri, has earned a college degree and now teaches. As part of her undergraduate work, she wrote a paper about me and earned an A, though I've never read the paper.

One secretary I had, recommended by her previous employer, an internist, as "the best secretary I've ever had" did not work out. She had a problem that I don't believe would be picked up by routine screening. In performance she could go from Point A to Point B and back to Point A. When Point C was included, she was hopelessly lost. Working for an internist with 30-minute appointments, she had no problem at this leisurely pace. However, she could not handle phones ringing, or shorter appointment slots with patients' checking in and out. On what turned out to be her last day, she said that since it was beginning to rain, she was going out to close her car windows. That was the last I saw of her. She never came back.

One substitute secretary utilized for a few weeks when Barbara B. was on maternity leave did not work out so well either. When "forehead" was dictated she typed "forrid," obviously, a devotee of spell-it-like-it-sounds. I also think she was a follower of the TV show *The Addams Family*, as on a patient's chart when dictation, referring to a biopsy report, should have read, "more tissue may be required to establish diagnosis," was, instead, typed as "Morticia may be required . . . ."

THE CAR – THE CAR

When I entered the examining room with a new patient waiting and introduced myself, he promptly asked what kind of car I drove. Having outside windows, great for a dermatologist, I pushed the curtain aside and pointed out my Volkswagen in the parking lot. He gave me permission to continue with the office visit. Seems he'd had it with doctors having His & Hers Porches, Jaguars and Cadillacs.

He had a point, but this was still a unique screening technique.

Double 'trician

Several years ago, I attended a Pediatric Dermatology Conference in Georgia. In a panel discussion, a pediatrician mentioned that as a baby gift, he gave new parents dummy plugs to block unused electrical outlets, inferring that this would prevent burns and shocks when a child placed a metal object into such an outlet. Another pediatrician said, "Not so, it would take a metal object being inserted in both openings simultaneously to cause a problem. Another pediatrician asked, "How do you know that?" The rebuttal pediatrician said simply, "I was an electrician before I became a pediatrician."

Price is Right

I once asked a new patient how he came to choose me. He said he had called all the dermatologists' offices in Lexington, and as my fees were the lowest, he had chosen me. I responded by thanking him for choosing me, but didn't think using that basis a proper way to choose a good restaurant.

Smart Alec Doc
The Author

As I walked into the examining room, my assigned Family Practice resident close behind, the patient, a boy of ten or twelve years of age was sitting on the side of the examining table, his left shoe and sock off readily revealing the dermatitis across the top of his foot. His father was seated in the spare examining room chair. I introduced myself, then the resident, or it could have been the other way around, and immediately asked, "When did you all get back from Florida?"

The father said, "About two weeks ago," and I favored the awed resident with a faint smile. He was thinking, "How did the doc know they had been to Florida? He didn't know them till now."

Then the father shot me out of the saddle saying, "He had the rash before we went to Florida."

UH-OH!

But I knew the second question to ask, "Where were you before you went to Florida?"

He said, "Panama," and then I could smile again. The youngster had cutaneous larva migrans, which is contracted, in warm weather areas, i.e. Florida, tropics. Most of the folks in Kentucky, if they get it, bring it home from Florida with them from their vacation. The characteristic skin pattern is that of a cat or dog hookworm wandering in a foreign host and is easily treated.

The resident was still impressed.

TIM CONWAY SPECIAL

I saw a quite elderly lady one day, and I think this great comedian must have seen this dear lady or one just like her. She walked just like the elderly people in the Conway skit, talked like them, looked like them. In this day of political correctness, we need a disclaimer here. If we are fortunate to live long enough, many of us may be just like that. So what! Anyhow, this lady, with hair like Tim Conway's mop, came in because of a lesion on her arm. It appeared to be an early skin cancer. I so advised the patient, and she wanted it removed. These were the days before segregating needles and syringes from other used office refuse. I used a local anesthetic to anesthetize the area for removal, had already injected the area, and withdrawn the needle when about the time the used needle and syringe hit the bottom of the waste receptacle, she said in a long drawn out way with a shaky voice, "Ooooouch!" I tell you, it was several seconds, the longest delayed response to an injection, I'd ever heard.

After the lesion was in the specimen bottle and the removal area on her arm dressed, I told her that I'd like to see her in six months. In the way she said it, I knew what she meant when she said with halting words, "I – may – not – be – here – then." Six months would have been mid-winter and folks in Kentucky, at least a lot of them, go to Florida then. I chose to misunderstand and thus said, "Oh, you'll be in Florida?"

And pointing to the ceiling she said again in her halting way, "No, I – hope – to – be – up – there."

In case you wonder, she did come back in six months.

"*I*'s Been Watchin' You!"

An elderly man came in one day and his problem was shockingly severe leg ulcers with massive drainage. He had facial tissues tucked in the top of his socks to catch this drainage. With an internist to manage his diabetes, we were able to effect a prompt response, and his legs cleared quite promptly for which he was exceedingly grateful.

He was soon ready for dismissal, and as I finished giving him maintenance therapy instructions, he said to me, "Doc, *I*'s been *watchin*' you."

I replied, "Yes, Sir, and what have you seen?"

He replied, "The high point in *yo* day, *ain't* at the end of it when you *goes* to the bank, is it?"

This remains my all time favorite compliment and though I never saw him again, and he is doubtless now deceased, I shall never forget his gracious, meaningful accolade.

Sack Lunches
Food for the Skin

Having a pharmacy background, I formulated a line of acne medicines including soap, nighttime medicine, astringents, as well as special shampoos, and lotions, which I used in management of various common disorders. Frequently, patients would voice a note of appreciation that these were not only effective, but also reasonably priced, compared to the alternatives from the giant drug companies.

Mention of these medicines brings to mind an incident involving a patient who complained, oh, so politely! With the extensive acne patient census and consequent large requirements of medicines furnished for these patients, I found it expedient to have these three basic medicines prepackaged. This was done neatly using small brown paper bags for this purpose.

On a "bad day" when I had fallen behind schedule and patients were waiting longer than usual, a farmer was ushered into an examining room. He had seen these prepared "acne kits" in the secretary's area while in the waiting room. Upon my entrance into his presence, he asked, "Doc, is them brown paper bags, sack lunches for us *that has* had to wait so long?"

THE SOAP DOCTOR

Once when Judy, having experienced an episode of double vision, was referred by our family ophthalmologist (Dr. J. G.) for an evaluation to a consulting physician to whom she had not previously been, and subsequently, had to fill out the requisite information for establishing a patient record for her, one of the office personnel recognized my name on Judy's form as the same name as that of her dermatologist.

She, wishing to verify if, indeed, the Dr. Marsh listed on the form was the Dr. Marsh whom she knew, asked, "Is this Dr. Marsh, the dermatologist, THE SOAP DOCTOR, who has an office up on Nicholasville Road at Medical Heights?"

After Judy's assurance that they were one and the same, the young lady who exhibited a beautiful velvety complexion proceeded to do a commercial for "Dr. Marsh's Soap," reminiscent of the old commercials for detergents in years past.

She gained the attention of her fellow office colleagues, stating, "This is my dermatologist's wife, you know, the one I told you about, the one who has that wonderful soap."

Then turning back to Judy asked, "What kind of soap is that? What is in it?" And without waiting for Judy's reply, continued, "It is WONDERFUL. I use it on my husband's back, on my baby, on my face. It really does a splendid job."

Judy's suggestion to me was that, should I ever decide to market the soap via television, the young lady would be the natural star for the "soap commercial."

This incident brings to mind a second story in regard to my medicines, which involved one of many phone calls, which I have received subsequent to my retirement. After all these years – 12 plus – I still receive about one call per month.

Judy fielded one such call, and the young lady, aged 40, asked Judy where she might obtain the "Dr. Marsh astringent and soap." She further confessed to my wife that when she had learned of my impending retirement, that she had bought up a supply to last until she turned 40, she erroneously thinking that at that stage in her life, she would no longer require the medications. When, to her dismay, she learned that the line of products had been "retired" with the developer, she was in distress, and pleaded that I please reintroduce the products on the market, stating that she had lots of family members who would be willing to purchase them also.

I treasure these informal tributes to my practice of dermatology, and I thank these unnamed patients for their praise, their trust, and their confidence in my abilities.

Postscript to Private Practice

While the practice of medicine furnishes the ultimate in psychic income, it also makes possible, if one wishes, the financial ability to travel, educate one's children in private schools, collect art, or pursue other interests. It cannot, however, substitute for a broken relationship. As in all divorces, there is fault enough to be shared by both parties. My 29-year marriage to Elisabeth ended in 1982. All who have experienced this event will agree to the enormous feeling of guilt, loss, and failure one experiences. It is not the end of the world, it just feels like it is, and it feels this way for a long, long time.

"Time heals everything." No, it doesn't, but it makes reality bearable, and the old Arabic expression, "This too shall pass," comes into play.

EATING LESSON

In those years between my first and second marriages, I was eating the evening meal sitting at the counter at Frisch's. As I was eating, some of the food fell from my fork into my lap, and I thought, unnoticed by the gentleman sitting next to me. Not so, as it turned out, as this stranger commented in the form of a question, "Been feeding yourself long?

MARRIAGE

In 1987, I married Judy Hopkins, a schoolteacher in Bardstown, Kentucky. I had known her for a couple of years, but I did not date her until late 1986, about three days before the beginning of the New Year. We came from strongly similar backgrounds, and her brother, Jerry, had been one of my brother's students when he was professor at Southwestern Baptist Theological Seminary. There were also other co-incidental, or in Presbyterian theology, divinely appointed, connections in that my technician Pat Thomas had known her for years though I did not know that when I first dated her. My nurse, Sue, ever watchful over me, (and I, her senior) decided to check Judy out, getting her husband, an assistant school superintendent, to call Judy's principal, to see if "she was as represented."

Judy's principal set the record straight, when in answer to the question at hand replied," If he's just half as good a person as she, then he'll be OK."

Things moved along well and we were married by Jerry April 4, 1987, a month before her birthday, in a private ceremony. I used to hear married couples say that they had never had an argument, but I never believed them. However, it is true of our marriage. We do things together and are a devoted couple. Judy finished her teaching year at Bardstown and then taught at Scott County High School until her retirement in 1997.

*Mr. & Mrs. Berl (Ruth) Hopkins, at their
fiftieth wedding anniversary luncheon in
Lexington, Kentucky, September 6, 1994.
They are parents of Judy Hopkins Marsh.
Use of photo by permission of Tom Barnett
Phtotography*

*Glenn with father-in-law, Berl Hopkins,
on Father's Day, 1998*

Glenn and Judy, wedding picture, April 4, 1987

LIFE IN KENTUCKY

Almost from day one in Kentucky, I have been intrigued, amused, surprised, inspired, and impressed by the people of this state with whom I have come in contact. My earliest memories of my exposure to the natives of this state were pleasant, and I found myself thinking more and more about living here. When I finished my dermatology residency in Texas, I, thus, made it known that I would like to be stationed in Kentucky for my obligatory pay back time to the Army.

Happily, this wish came true, to the extent that I cannot imagine having lived anywhere else during the closeout of my military career, and the opening of my office for the private practice of dermatology. I have truly become a Kentuckian.

The following recountings of incidents and memories of the intriguing, the amusing, the surprising, and the inspiring are illustrative of my Kentucky and my fellow Kentuckians.

ALL IN THE SOUND

I had not been in Lexington very long when I noted a muffler problem in my car. One day in the office, a knowledgeable patient suggested that I take it to Jack's Tar Company on a certain street. I thought, at the time, that mufflers and paving or roofing were an odd combination. I drove up and down that street, almost ready to give up, when I spotted the business – Jack's Tire Company.

MIRACLE DRUG

Some few patients can be impossible. An example was the demanding middle-aged lady whom I saw as one of the first patients of the day. She called at noon to say indignantly that she was no better. I asked her if she'd had the prescription filled. An even more indignant "yes" was forthcoming. I then asked her if she'd taken the medicine. She answered, "No, not yet."

I don't believe she was quite as indignant with the last answer.

THE STACK CAKE

Pygmalion or Professor Higgins, I am not. Well, on second thought, I did take on the task of re-making my mother-in-law.

When I came into the Hopkins family as the sole son-in-law, my debut met with a mixed reception. Pop, as I have come to call my father-in-law over the years, seemed to take an immediate liking to the idea of having an ally on the scene and welcomed me unreservedly, but Ruth, (I didn't dare call her anything but Mrs. Hopkins at that time), on the other hand,

With Judy's parents, Ruth and "Pop" Hopkins

was quite reserved and looked at me with an almost-air of suspicion, even going as far as to say to Judy on one occasion before the wedding, of course, "Judy, we don't know that man." Never mind that she had been one of my patients and had made three or four visits to my office.

Needless to say, "Professor" Marsh here loved a challenge, so I set about winning her over. Progress was slow, but with a regular schedule of Friday night visits with the Hopkins clan, uncles, aunts, cousins, I slowly began my task. One never knew in those early days who would show up for those delicious suppers for which my mother-in-law was noted. Ruth, uncharacteristically, began to join in on the teasing more and more. I was making progress. There was tangible evidence when one Friday night, I was served the biggest piece of her famous chocolate pie, even bigger than Pop's piece of pie.

The real test of the transformation of this shy, reticent, country lady was revealed in its full splendor on one of those Friday nights shortly after Ruth's birthday in September. When Judy and I arrived, there was just a sprinkling of the rest of the extended family present, and Ruth was delighted with the outcome of another of her famous desserts, an old-fashioned apple stack cake that was on the menu for the evening. Judy and I had just bought her a special pan for baking the layers of the cake, and she wanted us to know that she was appreciative, and that our gift had contributed to the success of her culinary efforts that evening.

As a preface to what was to be a thank you for our gift, Ruth announced to the crowd, "This" – referring to the cake on display – "is the best thing I've ever made."

Now, I've never been one to miss an opportunity and Ruth had just opened the door of opportunity. I put a sly, slightly salacious grin on my face, sidled up close to Judy and glancing back and forth between the cake and Judy, said to Ruth, "Noooo, that's not the best thing you've ever made."

Ruth, suddenly flustered, and at a momentary loss for words stammered, "Uh, uh, I mean the best thing that was fun!"

There was the expected peal of laughter from the family, and Ruth joined in with her now characteristic soft chuckle. I was proud of my creation, and I can now get away with calling her Ruth.

Have a Seat

After the first round of chairs – modern made – in my waiting room failed the test, I bought some semi-antique or even mismatched, antique chairs, covered the seats with horsehide, and forgot about them. They lasted and lasted and lasted. One day my secretary overheard two elderly ladies discussing them as one said, "Look at these old chairs. Bet he didn't pay over five dollars a piece for them."

I remarked that if a similar conversation happened again that she suggest that I was still in the market for five-dollar chairs. At this time, they are still being used in my home lasting through the years in the office and now twelve years into retirement.

Absentee Sweating

One hot summer day on the farm when I was mowing and working on the road frontage, a big Lincoln sedan stopped and a young man dismounted and came over to the work area. He asked for directions to which I responded. He then said, "You don't remember me, do you?" I acknowledged that I didn't, and he refreshed my memory telling me that he was Dr. Mooney's houseboy and had served me when I had lunch there. I then remembered him and said, "I'll bet you have never seen Dr. Mooney sweat like this.

He replied, "No, suh, if there's any sweating done there, I's the one what does it!"

DIFFERENT STROKES FOR DIFFERENT FOLKS

I saw people from all walks of life who had all sorts of vocations. Here are two examples: the first represents an owner/proprietor of an ice-cream store. I always tried to talk to people about their vocations so I asked him if he liked his work and he replied, "I love it!"

I said, "Why do you like having your ice cream store?"

His reply, "The next time you're in one, notice the look on the customers' faces when the ice cream cone is handed them. They always smile. I love seeing people smile."

The second concerned a late middle-aged fellow who was a farmer, a Jewish farmer, in fact. I remarked that to the best of my memory, he was the first Jewish farmer I had ever met.

He said, "Well, I wasn't always a farmer. I was a jeweler for a number of years and now I'm a farmer."

I said, "How interesting and what do you grow on your farm?"

Even more startling he said, "Pigs."

Seeing the expression on my face in responses to his answer, he said, "It's OK, Doc, they're Kosher."

MR. BYRD

Mr. Byrd was a longtime patient who, when he arrived for his appointment, brightened the entire office. He was elderly, with a shock of snow-white hair, well-groomed, and dressed almost always in a suit or in color-coordinated attire. He projected the image of a gentleman of the old school with his fluent speech and his courteous manner. His timing of the lines of a story would match Bob Hope's best. During the last time I saw him he said, "I've reached that point in life when I want to know the answer to three questions: Number one, where are my glasses? Number two, where is the bathroom? and Number three –uh? and uh Number three, uh, uh, uh? number three, number three? – I can't remember."

I miss him greatly.

SMALL WORLD #2

During World War II, my oldest brother, Ralph, a veterinarian served in the China-Burma-India (CBI) theater of operations. Most of the time, he was in or about Karachi. He was an avid hunter, and while I don't remember his various hunting adventures, I do remember receiving, from that far off land, a package, which contained a bearskin rug. This is the background to "the rest of the story."

In the 1970s, the building where my office was located was severely damaged by fire. This fire originated upstairs near a psychiatrist's office with the major burn damage there. However, my office downstairs near the other end of the building experienced mainly water and smoke damage. This damage compelled us to move a few blocks away to a temporary location while the original medical building was being repaired and renovated. This was my first experience with fire.

Late one morning in the second office location, I had finished with the last patient and while he dressed, I retired to my office to go through the mail.

As I sat there opening the mail, he half entered my office saying, "I hear you are interested in guns and hunting." I acknowledged that I was much more of a target shooter than hunter, but did some hunting.

He wanted my opinion on buying one rifle that would be adequate for big game the size of deer, but could also be used for varmints, i.e. groundhogs, crows. I made a suggestion and he asked me a technical question or two, and it seemed to me he would be planning on more projected use for deer hunting than the other, so I commented that while a 30-06 caliber would be excellent for deer, it was a bit much for the groundhog aspect. At this point he said, "A doctor I was with in the Army had a bear chase him up a tree, and he had to shoot it multiple times at close range with a 30-06." My memory kicked in and I said, "He was in India – a veterinarian from Alabama, my brother."

The patient, J. B., was astonished at these facts and only then realized the name connection.

This patient died about two years ago (2000).

A poor tanning and taxidermy job resulted in the bearskin rug's being thrown away many, many years ago.

SUSPICIOUS CHARACTER

One day during lunch hour, I walked less than one-half block over to Circuit City to obtain a replacement part for my home stereo. A gentleman waited on me, obtained the part for me and during the conversation, called me by name, remarking that he had seen me once as a patient with an infection involving the skin of his face. He added that the antibiotics prescribed cleared the infection promptly and that he was pleased with the results. We made our way to the cash register where I wrote the firm a check for $26 whereupon he asked to see some ID.

Rules supersede reason.

CLOTHES MAKE THE MAN

This story was related to me by my niece, Dr. Martha Marsh, of Birmingham, Alabama, having heard it from Polly, a colleague of hers with whom she taught in Alabama many years ago, but who now lives in Kentucky. It seems this lady, who told Polly of the incident, was on her way to her daughter's orthodontist, with the daughter and another of her children. Unfortunately, her car stalled on the south side of Lexington, and as the car sat on the side of the road and as she was wondering what to do, an old unshaven, raggedly dressed farmer, driving a Cadillac stopped, asking if he could be of assistance. She described her plight, mentioning with growing apprehension that it was approaching the time for her daughter's appointment. The farmer said he'd help; bade the mother and two girls enter the car, drove them to a repair facility, helped make arrangements for towing the car, and then drove to his nearby home, got out, leaving the keys in the ignition, telling the lady to bring the car back when she was through with it, and he would take her back to the garage to pick up her car. The lady seemed to think this somewhat remarkable.

I didn't; I learned a long time ago, that it is truly more blessed to give than to receive, and I believe giving includes the giving of one's service, not just tangible items.

A word of explanation is in order. I am not a Cadillac person. My Buick had been totaled by one of my sons and being a proponent of buying used cars, I delayed too long in looking for a replacement Buick and could not find what I wanted. One of my patients had lost her husband and his Cadillac was for sale. I bought it, my first and last Cadillac. I never felt comfortable in that car, my being a Ford or Chevy – one-time Buick person – later a Honda person. Besides, that 1975 Cadillac was not satisfactory. Its performance matched its lemon color.

How Often is Often Enough?

After I entered practice, I spent several Thursday afternoons calling on physicians in towns and cities surrounding Lexington in an attempt to get to know these *front-line* doctors and hopefully, attract some referrals. In general, the time was well spent, and I made some really good friends and picked up a story or two that I have never forgotten. This one is from my visit in 1968 with Dr. Arch Clark, now retired, of Richmond, Kentucky, home of Eastern Kentucky University.

The young mother who was in for her six-weeks postpartum exam, which was normal, wished advice relative to birth control methods. After hearing an explanation of the methods available, she decided upon the "pill." Dr. Clark, having a package readily available for demonstration, showed her the card with a tablet to be taken everyday. At this point, she stopped him, and with her gaze directed downward to the floor, said with some embarrassment, "Doctor, we won't need one that often."

Just Like Home

The practitioner should never be surprised at what patients
notice about his office. A sweet country woman once told me,
"You have the homiest [maybe she actually said *homeliest*] office
I ever was in. If you just had a *chimley*, it would be perfect."

The Things Your Patients Say About You

For a few years after entering practice in Lexington, I was a
member of the active U.S. Army Reserve. This, along with moonlighting at the local health department, brought in some needed
added income during the time my practice was building. We
went to camp for two weeks in the summer and had drill, not
actually, but that is what it was called, one weekend monthly.
On those weekends, we did physical exams for promotion, en-
listment, and other reasons. Both officers and enlisted men wore
nametags, and I spotted a former patient in line to get his physical
for induction into the reserve unit. When his turn came, he sat
down across the table before me. I positioned a manila folder in
front of my nametag and proceeded with my part of the physical, which involved taking the medical history of the applicant.
As I began the questioning, he still had not recognized me though
I reviewed in detail his history and saw on his papers where he
had listed my name as a physician he had consulted during the
last two years. I said, "Tell me about your visit with this Marsh
fellow." He related accurately the details of his visit. Temptation
was overpowering and I succumbed saying, "We don't think
very much of this Marsh guy around here. We think that he is
just one-half step from being a quack."

This young man bristled, sat quite erect in his chair and
said, "Sir, I don't think that's fair. I went to him and he did a
good job for me and was fair in every respect."

I could suppress my deception no longer, and breaking into
a wide grin, [I like to think that's why he didn't recognize me,
because of my stern military visage instead of the usual grin], I
lowered my manila folder to reveal my name. When he finally

recognized me, he too broke into a solid laugh. I got in the last word, as I usually do, "We're going to let you in this *medical unit*, but you can forget about the CIC (Counter Intelligence Corps).

They Did That Back Then?

Language has a way of dating one, and helping to create that gulf known as the "generation gap."

My wife, Judy, was reminded of this fact by a humorous happening in her freshman English class a few years ago as she was teaching Shakespeare's *Romeo and Juliet*.

One bright-eyed freshman asked, "What's wrong with Romeo at the beginning of the play?"

Judy explained, "Romeo, who has not yet seen Juliet, thinks he is in love with Rosaline and he's 'love struck.'" As is characteristic of my wife, she thought it necessary to enlighten the class in regard to the term "love struck" with a clearer explanation so she continued, "He's 'mooning' over Rosaline."

Coming from a generation that had never heard the term "mooning" used in this classical sense, this young, incredulous freshman, asked, "They did that back then?"

The whole class erupted in a gale of laughter, as did the teacher, who then attempted to close the generation gap by explaining that *mooning* in this sense means, "exhibiting infatuation." The freshmen were greatly disappointed to learn that Romeo was not of their generation.

Only Two Moons

Speaking of that not too genteel tradition of "mooning," as the younger generation defines the word, a story told by L. B., a close teacher friend of Judy's and now of mine goes something like this: L. was driving the cheerleader's van and was passing the player's bus when three of her cheerleaders, two white and one black, decided to moon the team as they passed. L. later noted that when she charged them with the offense of mooning, the three of them informed her that she was wrong – there were only two moons. The third, they insisted, was an eclipse.

HOLIDAY JOY

My wife, teacher of A. P. Senior English, assigned a theme dealing with the Christmas/New Years' Holidays. A passage from one of these student papers stated, "How wonderful it was to be at Grandmother's house on Christmas enjoying all that *fudge* and *virginity*!

HOME SWEET HOME

Another theme assignment of descriptive character, emphasizing the use of spatial description, when describing the contents of a room stated, "Chester's drawers was standing in the corner!"

ADOLPH RUPP

It was my good fortune, though I was apprehensive at the time, to have Coach Adolph Rupp as a patient. Legion were the stories of this renowned person. It was a given that he was a taskmaster, uncompromising in his approach to the game of basketball, according to some, a tyrant who was intolerant of people in general. Well, at least, that was what I had heard. At home, bedridden, recuperating from emergency surgery performed in Nashville where UK had played Vanderbilt, he called me one day. He was displeased with his current dermatologist and plainly, though not unkindly, told me so. With misgivings, I agreed to make a house call at the end of my day in the office. I don't know, probably have simply forgotten, where he got my name. Thinking that this old man would be telling me how, what, and when to do, I looked upon the scheduled visit as more unfortunate than fortunate!

I was never more wrong. This patient was cooperative to a fault and allowed me to call the shots without a murmur of distrust or question. His response was prompt and complete, and he became one of the most appreciative patients that I have ever had. He looked for ways to express his appreciation, and I found myself dropping by more than once to enjoy his conversation and wit. I found the whole family, Mrs. Rupp, son Herky, daugher-in-law, Linda, and his two grandchildren, Farren and Chip to be warm and gracious. It saddens me that the accusation "racist" arises from time to time in reference to Coach Rupp. All I can say is that in my numerous conversations with Coach Rupp, there was never a hint of this.

Knowing that I was not a devotee of basketball, he once called to advise that he was leaving tickets at the box-office so I could see the greatest basketball player he had ever seen play the game, "Dr. J." I had never seen before or since any quote of Coach Rupp wherein he referred to the greatest basketball player he had ever seen. People that I consider racists would never acknowledge that someone not of their race were the best in any endeavor.

Everyone who knew him seemed to have a favorite Coach Rupp story. This one was told me by team physician Dr. Vance Jackson from Paducah. When Coach Rupp was new in his job as basketball coach at UK, the pay was not too good, so he officiated at high school games on Friday nights to earn extra income. Coach made some unpopular calls that offended the partisan home crowd, and when the game was over, he was accosted by a big, really big man, who proceeded to give Coach Rupp a piece of his mind. Coach Rupp interrupted him saying, "Mister, what do you do for a living?"

The irate fan replied, "I'm a farmer."

Coach Rupp in that distinctly flat voice, but sharp-tongued way of his said, "I thought so. Tomorrow, you'll be back shoveling manure, and I'll be back coaching basketball, which is what I do for a living!"

I was sitting next to Coach Rupp at one of the Kentucky Colonels' professional basketball games and people brought all manner of items, some trash, food containers, to be autographed. I asked him if he didn't tire of signing *stuff*?

"Yeh, I do," he replied, "but when they quit asking for your name, you're dead."

My favorite recollection of Coach Rupp involved my mother who was visiting in Lexington from Auburn, Alabama, no slouch of a sports town itself. My mother loved all sports, whatever was in season and in fact, as she passed away, the radio in her hospital room was tuned to some sporting event and her last words were, "What's the score?"

On the occasion of this visit, my mother and I were in attendance at another Kentucky Colonels' game where we sat at one end of the row with Coach Rupp and his entourage at the other end of the row. At half-time, I noticed him edge away from the notables in his presence. As he made his way toward my mother, he exclaimed as he greeted her, "Doctor, I want to meet your mamma." I thought my mother would swoon. I always thought this the high point of her fascination with sports and Coach Rupp's gracious demeanor was a far cry from all of the negative things that I continue to hear. This is but one example of his kindly actions toward my family and me.

Being one of the team doctors during three basketball coaches' tenure and three football coaches' tenure, all of whom I knew personally, I found none of those gentlemen anywhere nearly so gracious to me as Coach Rupp.

I liked him – I liked him very much.

A Diner's Advice

When being visited by Faye and Felix Sandlin, friends from San Antonio, we took them to Claudia Sander's Dinner House. This burned in 1999, is now rebuilt and is/was a great place to "pig out." Featured items on the menu are Kentucky country ham and fried chicken. Also, prominent among the culinary delights are/were luscious homemade yeast rolls, served by a roaming waiter/waitress who goes from table to table during the course of the evening, and nine vegetables served family style.

During our dinner, this waiter brought each of us a roll, which we all made disappear as if by magic. There seemed to be more of a delay for his return for a second serving than I thought reasonable, so when he did return, I chided him in a pleasant sort of way saying, "Son, where have you been? If you keep bringing these rolls, I may place you in my will." Turning to my wife I said, not in an unduly loud voice, "I'd like to come here sometime and forget about these nine veggies and eat all of the country ham and these rolls they'll bring me."

A voice from across the room replied, "You do that and they'll be reading your will before you're ready." After a good laugh, I then ate my veggies without comment when he informed me that he had recently had bypass surgery and thus, I learned the reason for his warning.

Maury Kaufmann, MD

Maury Kaufmann, MD, good friend of many years, now deceased, came to Kentucky from Philadelphia and was in general practice in Eastern Kentucky for years about which he wrote a delightful autobiographical book concerning the Jewish doctor from the big city who came to a rural state and how he had to learn the culture from the ground up.

Whenever Maury came to the office, I would always get off schedule, as we would swap stories and jokes. One of my favorites told in Maury's best, only slightly exaggerated Philly accent, concerned the Jewish husband who went to see his physician. When he returned home, his wife asked about the visit. The husband replied that his doctor thought, "It could be serious, might be herpes." She excused herself and returned with a medical book in hand saying, "Get yourself another doctor. This book says that herpes is a disease of the (G)entiles."

As a tribute to this great physician, the building which houses Hospice of the Bluegrass was named in his honor. I miss

Maury as well as many others who always brought at least a smile, more often a belly laugh to the office. Not all of Maury's jokes were G-rated, but all were funny, and I never detected one hint of a mean spirit in this kind, gentle, funny man.

I loved him!

DID I REALLY DO/SAY THAT?

When Judy and I were courting and I had been to her apartment and served a wonderful meal, the dishes cleared away, and now sitting very close together, the lights turned low, soft romantic music playing, and we were saying those wonderfully romantic things to each other, how in the world did I call her by a former girlfriend's name? Dead, dead, dead silence. One could have heard a handkerchief hit the floor. It really wasn't all that long, but seemed to be. I apologized profusely from the northern, eastern, southern, and western approaches and her response was a classic, causing me to know for certain that she was the girl for me. She said, "That's all right, George."

MISS AMERICA

One day Miss America came to my office as a patient. Well, she really wasn't Miss America, had no chance of even being Miss Jessamine County, Kentucky whence she had come, but because of her endearing qualities, she would have gotten my vote.

I don't recall, this event having been many years ago, the circumstances of her appointment – whether referred from her family doctor, though I think this the most likely, or if she came upon advice of a friend or family, or just "walked in." I do remember it was a cooler month, probably autumn. She was wearing a nondescript blouse, a faded unevenly hemmed skirt – too long for accepted style, and rough, oversized shoes called brogans in my early years. Her coat, with its lining hanging out in the back, was obviously a hand-me-down, too large, and possibly one outgrown by her brother. The apparel, while shabby, was clean. She wore no makeup, her hair was neatly combed, she had a nice complexion, pretty smile, and her face sort of glowed both from the well-scrubbed texture and most significantly from an inner charm or as I tend to refer to this as "presence."

Her dermatologic problem required a second visit (no charge was assessed on either). I did not charge her for two reasons. First, it was evident that she had no money and secondly, I suspect, just about know, that she would not have returned for the needed follow-up visit had she been charged for the first visit.

She returned in two weeks as scheduled having improved very nicely. I had furnished her needed medicines from samples. Her dress was almost the same as before, and as I was dismissing her from my care, I took a moment to get to know her better. Since her appointment was right after lunch, I asked if she were returning to school. I don't remember her age, but do recall that she was not yet eighteen. She replied, "No, I'm going to help my daddy cut postes," Kentucky plural for fence posts, a grueling, hard, exhausting job even for a young, athletically inclined man. In the manner of her reply, there was no resentment or resignation. In fact, there was a hint, in the way she said, "Daddy," as to her affection for him.

As a judge of Miss America, Jr. Miss, or Teenage Miss America, I couldn't rank her "swimsuit" as her attire precluded any assessment of her figure, and post cutting wasn't a permitted category in the talent competition, but for this judge, her bearing, character, personal appearance, and acceptance of family responsibility including work sharing, carried the day.

I never saw her again, but I remember her once or twice a year and wonder now that she is approaching age forty, how life has worked out for her as an unrecognized Miss America. I should mention that she had trimmed her clean fingernails very short, not from biting, and that she had work-hardened hands showing abrasions and cuts.

The World's Greatest, Last Bologna Sandwich

About five years ago, there was an article in the Lexington paper about a little grocery store that was going out of business as soon as the last of their current stock of this special bologna was sold. This was just the sort of ad to attract a husband and a wife on a snow day with nothing better to do, so we went. We had no trouble finding this one-room diamond in the rough. No other customers were there, even though it was about the time that the home folks would be thinking about their stomachs. We went in and we were really in luck. The elderly lady said she had only enough bologna for just two sandwiches.

"We'll take it!"

Looked and smelled like generic bologna to me, I know the bread wasn't anything special since we'd left a loaf in the kitchen with the same brand wrapper on it. The only choice of drink was milk, sold out of everything else. I then spotted a box of Moon Pies. "Take two of those." Judy didn't know about Moon Pies and afterwards she was to learn that the knowledge wasn't particularly flavorful – a marshmallow between two wafers but still the stuff of epic southern folklore if consumed with an RC Cola, pronounced 'aura cee." The world's greatest bologna sandwich?

Baloney!

Sidebar: Kentucky has some strange pronunciations: Versailles is pronounced "Ver-sales" and Athens uses a long "a." You figure it out. Also, geographically, West Liberty, Kentucky is east of Liberty, Kentucky.

Seat Belts

My elderly next door neighbor and I had some business to transact in nearby Versailles, Kentucky. I agreed to pick him up and after he had seated himself, I suggested he "buckle up." He was resistant to the idea, and when I repeated the suggestion, he again refused. Upon the third try, he said, "I don't believe in them things. If we have a wreck and the car 'ketches on far,' I'll burn up."

I pointed out that only a fraction of one-percent of auto accidents result in fire, but he again refused.

As we drove along the unfamiliar winding back road, I was engrossed in conversation and allowed the vehicular speed to be greater than ideal for this road. We abruptly came upon a sharp, right-angle turn with a gravel lane proceeding straight ahead just as the main road began this sharp turn. It was evident that I would not be able to make the curve, so I continued straight on down the lane a short distance stopping in a shower of gravel and a cloud of dust.

My neighbor after regaining his breath, remarked dryly, "I see now why **you** need them *thar* seat belts."

A BIG FAT ONE

I don't know why, but my two favorite patient groups were teenagers (and younger) and elderly patients, especially farmers.

Bert Wheeler was from Somerset, Kentucky and brightened the day for all of us when he came in. Mr. Wheeler had a recurring skin problem related to his prolonged sun exposure as a farmer and came about twice yearly and customarily spoke in a loud voice even in a one-on-one situation. Not only did he speak loudly, but also he had a high-pitched voice, which made for an even louder, or at least, more penetrating voice.

On this particular day when he arrived, he announced to the receptionist, and this included everyone in the whole office suite, the fact that he had brought me a chicken. In an equally penetrating voice, he related that his wife had admonished him saying, "If you're going to take that doctor a chicken, you take him a big fat one." I was told that he held up the picked chicken by the neck so that all in the waiting room could admire his poultry and verify what those of us in the examining rooms had already heard.

BARN BUILDER

In 1972, a series of tornadoes swept across Kentucky laying waste to property, especially barns, mobile homes, and in some cases, an entire area, i.e. Jett, Ky.

Along with many others, I lost a tobacco barn and found myself in a mad scramble to build a new replacement barn. There was also a shortage of building materials, coupled with a compressed span of time from tobacco plant setting time to harvest, and most of all, a shortage of experienced barn builders.

As usual, my approach was to study the problem, so I enlisted the aid of the University of Kentucky Agriculture department and after consultation, decided that the best barn would be a pole barn, which would be more labor efficient in housing the tobacco crop. I heard about a barn builder in a not too distant county and somehow found his isolated-and-without-telephone home. When I arrived, I noticed the license plate on the front bumper of the car in the yard proclaimed, "Eat more beans, we need the gas!" The owner of the car, an unkempt young man, shirtless and with his arm in a soiled cast, supported by a sling, had a tattoo over each nipple, one stating *Hot* and the other *Cold*. The barn builder came through the front door opening, then pushed open the screen door, said screen not attached except to the lower half of the door and the door itself swung on one hinge only. I was asked whether I wanted to come inside to talk or would I rather talk outside. The outside being a known quantity was definitely preferred. I told the barn builder the type of barn I had decided upon and handed him the four pages of blueprints. He studied each page minutely, running his index finger, showing much real estate under his fingernail, line by line across the plans. For some five minutes, the study continued in silence, and when at last, his study completed, I asked if he could build such a barn. Without hesitation, he assured me that he could, exactly, per plans.

I then asked him what kind of barn he preferred, i.e. the kind that he usually built. He told me in a sentence or two, and I immediately stated that I'd prefer his style barn be built for me. You see, I'd noticed that his detailed study was with the blueprints upside down. He was illiterate. Can you imagine what the barn would have looked like built with his interpretation of the plans?

He built the barn and it is still standing.

STEREOTYPING
CARS MAKE THE DOCTOR

Once on a late Saturday afternoon on the way home from the farm, I stopped by Central Baptist Hospital to check on a patient. My Ford station wagon was slightly, well, to be honest, considerably on the disreputable looking side, and besides that, it was stuffed with farm tools, plows, chain saw, and weed eater. I pulled, as usual, into the physician's parking lot and went in to see my patient.

When I came out of the hospital, there was a neat but very indignant note under the windshield wiper. "Do not park here again. This space is reserved for doctors."

NO PAIN ZONE

Dermatologists see a lot of patients with warts. I was no exception. They're frustrating – they're frequently uncommonly difficult to remove, but happily, they're benign. Understandably, patients want them to be gone and to be gone promptly.

A mother brought in her son, about twelve or fourteen years of age, with a wart involving the margin of the thumbnail on his right hand. This is a particularly painful area to treat, but we use liquid nitrogen, freezing the wart to approximately 323 degrees below zero, and usually this will suffice, but not always. I found that a freeze, and then allowing it to thaw, and then to re-freeze, all on the first visit yielded better results than a simple one-time freezing.

I froze the youngster's wart, told him that it would really hurt when it thawed out, but that it would not hurt so badly if he held his thumb above the level of his heart, and as I prepared to leave the room, I said, but should not have, "The higher you hold your thumb above the heart, the less it will hurt."

When I came back into the room in about five minutes to refreeze it, I was astonished to see his mother reading the newspaper and son *standing* on the exam table with his thumb touching the ceiling. It had apparently not occurred to either of them that no matter where one stands, he can only get his thumb so far above the heart.

ANATOMY LESSON

The greatest putdown I ever received was from a four-year-old. Let me tell you about it. An intelligent, attractive young mother with a delightful youngster came into my office, and as was my usual custom, I sat down on the examining table beside her son, the patient. This allowed him to get used to me and over the years it worked well in dealing with children. He had a non-specific eruption involving the elbows and knees, and I explained to the mother that this was common in children and certain pediatricians thought it was a grass allergy, dermatologists thought it was, perhaps, the result of carpet irritation with the kids pushing the toys along on the carpeted floor and/or watching television, chin propped on elbows. I went on to say, "It is not serious. It really doesn't make that much difference as to the etiology because it will be gone in a matter of a few weeks, treated or untreated." And in sort of an eloquent flourish to complete discussion of the subject, I reached over, and as I tapped his knee where the rash was most prominent, I said, "We simply do not know what this is."

The kid looked up at me with an astonished look on his face and said,"It's a knee!"

'NUFF SAID

On another occasion, I entered the examining room and the six or seven-year-old patient was already sitting on the exam table. I greeted his mother, and in a departure from my usual approach asked this bright youngster, "What do you want to hear from me?"

Without hesitation, he replied, "It isn't serious, I don't need a shot, and come back in a year."

POSITIVE THINKING

My best, long-standing friend, Jack Adcock, is a gregarious person who never met a stranger that he didn't try to make into a friend. As a result, he sometimes "rushes in where angels fear to tread," and being around him is an experience in itself. In addition, he is physically quite strong, once twisting the handle off my new heavy-duty screwdriver in trying to remove a rusty

Glenn and Jack Adcock, my best, longtime buddy with whom I have shared many adventures and laughs. Jack is the most loyal friend ever. I love him. Photo, Lexington, Kentucky, 1989

screw. He and glass are somewhat incompatible. He once walked through a plate glass door, with only minor cuts as a result, and while browsing in a fashionable men's store, decided to seat the ground glass stopper of a cut glass whiskey decanter more deeply with a slap of his palm resulting in the the decanter's complete disintegration. At that point, I distanced myself from him in his time of need by pretending to be interested in apparel across the store from the decanter. He resolved his involvement with the decanter with the manager, and later as we walked through the mall, he intimated, "I believe it was already cracked."

It's the Thought That Counts

Jack's uncle was also named Jack and was well into his eighties and his wife, Aunt Izzy in her early eighties. Jack asked his Uncle Jack what he had had for supper the previous night. Uncle Jack replied, "Oysters."

My buddy, pressing the issue asked, "Did they do you any good?"

Uncle Jack replied, "I guess so; I thought about it."

Heavenly Sport

My former wife not only did not like sports, she could attend the most exciting sporting event and remain completely detached.

One beautiful third week in October, on a football Saturday, as my best friend, his wife, my ex, and I walked across the UK campus with the blue sky overhead that only a poet could describe, with leaves in full color, and a delightful nip in the air, I waxed eloquent saying to my friend (Jack Adcock), "Jack, I have it on good authority that there's a football game every Saturday afternoon, year-round in Heaven."

A millisecond later, my ex-wife authoritatively stated, "That wouldn't be Heaven, that would be Hell."

The sky was then of a paler blue, the leaves were just a touch faded. However, that nip in the air was accentuated by my ex-wife's chilly reception to my exuberant statement regarding fall and football.

SELF-MEDICATION

After I had prostate surgery, I shared a room, post surgery, with an elderly gentleman who had a permanent tracheostomy and also delusions of being poisoned. I didn't get any sleep as he paced the floor repeatedly, and about every hour would lightly pinch my big toe, I suppose, to see if I were still alive and kicking. I finally drifted off to sleep about four a.m., only to be awakened a short time later by a nurse's voice saying, "You did WHAT?"

With his tracheostomy, he had to resort to written notes. The nurse then said, "Just a minute," and left.

She was then replaced by a second nurse who seeing his written note said, "You did WHAT?" She also left.

The third nurse came in with a repeat of the above conversation.

The incredulous quotes were occasioned by the first nurse's coming in to replace his IV, and noting the full bottle, asked how this could be. The patient had written on his pad, "The IV was empty, so I went to the sink and refilled it from the faucet." This brought on the series of "You did WHAT?" each nurse having to hear, i.e. read the story before believing it. After the three gathered, they were then faced with the task of reassuring him that things would probably be all right, but "Don't do it again."

MY WIFE – MY DAUGHTER

When Judy and I were married in 1987, she was 39 and I was 57. This has caused, on occasion, some confusion as to whether this beautiful lady with me is my daughter or my wife. Charlie Haffner, a long time friend from Tennessee, after being introduced to Judy, looked her up and down, and in a very slow southern drawl remarked, "Well, good doctor, is she your wife or is she your daughter?" Knowing his personality, I was prepared to expect something like his question and thus, replied. "Charlie, she has to be my wife. I'm too old to have a daughter this young."

In character and with great emphasis, he replied, "Touché, good doctor, touché."

Before too long, I learned another way to handle inquisitive looks of the various people that took interest in our age difference. A remark going something on this order would usually suffice, "We are really the same age– the difference is she has had two, or is it three, face lifts?" Even that quip was sometimes inadequate as, for instance, once when giving a paper with Judy's being my projectionist, I made the above statement in a lull in an attempt to inject humor. After the presentation, one old man, about my age, after looking over her face carefully, said, "Whoever did it, did a good job. I don't see any scars."

BILINGUAL

In the early part of the last century, before the proliferation of radio and television, it was commonly held that the speech patterns/pronunciations of the isolated mountain folk were nearest to those of the Elizabethan period, Shakespeare's time and perhaps, even going back as far as the Middle English era, that of Geoffrey Chaucer. For example, on one occasion, I met a dear mountain lady, in her late eighties or early nineties, who regularly used the word "holpen" (Middle English) in place of "helped." Having always been interested in language, in general, and the dialects of people, in particular, I recalled an incident related by my parents in regard to a happening in the rural section of Alabama, which might just as well have happened in the mountainous area of Kentucky.

As the story goes, this backwoods kid was taken to the doctor by his parents. When the doctor said, "Stick out your tongue," he remained motionless. The doctor repeated this request with the same result. The doctor turned to the mother who interpreted, "Loll out your lolliper, son." And he promptly stuck out his tongue.

We, in the family, presumed this family to be a bit more ignorant than we were, but when I told this story to Judy Love, she mused, "Lolliper, lolliper, lolliper – lollipop," and proceeded to obtain the dictionary and found that lolliper is Middle English (northern dialect) for tongue.

Smart wife!

I Don't Care To

The following story is in the same vein. In Kentucky, at least in Rockcastle County, Kentucky, "I don't care to," has a special meaning, as much by inflection as by word. I had not been in the family long, when the ladies, at the last moment in preparing the meal, needed something, perhaps, a loaf of bread, and I said to Judy's father, "Pop, would you like to go to the store with me?"

He said, "I don't care to," and reached for his hat to accompany me. The local meaning of the phrase is interpreted as "I don't mind if I do," with an affirmative intonation.

Hotrod Honda

At the end of a crop year, I went to pick up an eighteen-foot piece of irrigating pipe lent to a farmer in the next county. Almost always when you lend something to a farmer, you have to go get it yourself. People lend me things, and they have to come get them too.

I used my Honda Prelude as the transport vehicle, straddling the pipe and securing it to the front and rear bumper, with it safely slung below the car. I parked the car in the drive upon return. Someone later parked behind, with the direct rear of the Honda presented, and seeing the end of the six inch diameter pipe extending just slightly to the rear of the bumper, asked, "What kind of muffler is **that**?"

You Can't Please Everybody

One day a male patient, presenting with a large fungating skin lesion on his forearm, said, "I want this cancer removed."

I agreed with his diagnosis, saying that it was cancer till proved otherwise, and removed it forthwith. A few days later, the pathology report arrived and usually the nurse called to advise the patient if the lesion was benign. As a matter of policy, I usually called only when the report was other than benign, but I was so pleased for him, that I elected to call, and the conversation went something like this, "Mr. Morrow, I've called to give you the **good** news that the large growth that both of us thought to be cancer is not."

He replied curtly, "That's **not good** news! I've got a cancer policy, and now, it won't pay a dime."

I'm hardly ever at a loss for words. I was then.

Group Rate

My Old Kentucky Home at Bardstown, Kentucky is one of our favorite places to visit and when company came, especially from out of town, we would often take them for a visit to what we considered a nice slice of Kentucky. My first wife's sister and her husband with their six children came one summer, and with our four children, this made a sizable gang. We rang the bell for the tour guide to take us through the home, and as she opened the door and saw us clustered on the steps and sidewalk, she was visibly surprised saying, "Is this some kind of a group?"

I replied, "No, we're just good Catholics." Elisabeth's sister, brother-in-law, and all their children were good Catholics–Elisabeth and I and the children were just good.

Directions
Eastern Kentucky Style

A patient of mine, M.N., a psychologist at Eastern State Hospital here in Lexington, was invited to present a lecture at

Alice Lloyd College, a small school in a remote area of eastern Kentucky near the Kentucky-Virginia state line, at Pippa Passes, Kentucky.

He drove to this isolated area, gave his lecture, stayed longer than planned, and began his trip home. The "shadders," as they are called, lengthened and the "hills and hollers" seemed to be closing in as day was nearly done. The road did not look familiar; he saw no evidence of the road's being the one he had traveled but a few hours previously, so he decided to stop at the next available source for directions. Soon he came upon a crossroads emporium, one-pump, combination gas station and grocery – this one complete with a "happy pappy" sitting on the porch in a rocking chair. Happy pappy was a term, then used frequently, until about ten or so years ago to describe a person who had fathered numerous children, who would not work at an established job, and who took life, not very seriously, while awaiting the arrival of a welfare check. His personal appearance was characterized by a much-stained hat, boiled, once-white shirt buttoned at top of collar, shapeless suit coat with lining hanging out in back, three-four day growth of beard, edentulous or nearly so, tobacco-stained corners of mouth from snuff or chewing tobacco, bib overalls, and high topped, black tennis shoes without socks. Names differ for such a character from geographic area to geographic area, but the reader gets the idea.

M.N., my patient and my friend, came to a stop before this person, rolled down the window and asked in a voice loud enough for the occupant of the rocking chair to hear as he rocked, "How do you get to Lexington?"

Continuing to rock, the man in the chair replied, "My son-in-law; he takes me."

FAMILY VIGNETTES

Family has always been an important part of my life from the very earliest times to the current years, and while this writing includes various accounts of family interspersed throughout the other sections, I feel that I would be remiss were I not to recount the following random incidents/stories that are vivid and significant memories, many of which, I hope, will bring a smile to the reader or perhaps, bring to mind a fond memory of his/her own family members.

BEAUTIFUL EYES

In medical school one of the anatomy professors was markedly anti-God. He scarcely missed an opportunity to deride God. For instance, one day while lecturing on the anatomy of the eye, when summing up his opinion of the eye, he utilized a quote, "If I'd hired God to design the human eye, and he submitted what we have, I'd have fired him." Luckily, for all of us, this professor did not hear a fellow student who remarked under his breath, "The learned professor to whom this statement was attributed, died in his thirties."

Not too long afterward, when I made a visit to the anatomy building, I invited my six-year-old daughter to accompany me. As we made our way down the hall, I met and greeted this professor, and after speaking to me, he pleasantly asked who the young lady was who was accompanying me. I introduced

Ann and as she looked up at him, he was most impressed by her eyes and asked, "Where did you get those beautiful eyes?"

Without hesitation she replied, " God gave them to me."

Dr. Moore turned away, walked down the hall shaking his head as he went.

ADULT TRANSPORTATION

On another occasion when daughter Ann was about four years old, we went for a Sunday afternoon drive. We did not realize that she had never seen a wheelchair until when seeing one, she exclaimed excitedly, "Mother, look at the lady in that big stroller."

LIFE SAVERS

I don't remember exactly how it happened, but somewhere along the way my children and I, especially David, became very fond of Butter Rum Lifesavers. It was the flavor preferred on camping and hunting trips and in the car or truck on the way. I suppose it was a normal progression that when David gave me a yellow Labrador, to name her Butter Rum.

GRANDDAUGHTER'S SKIN OBSERVATION

My granddaughter, Mandy, at age four, observed the great number of wrinkles in her great-grandmother's face and asked, "Grandma, why does your face have so many curls?"

THE REAL DOCTOR

My daughter, Ann, age six, and I were on the way to Sunday school. I was a senior medical student at Emory University, and graduation was fast approaching. Ann had a loose front baby tooth, and she worried with it prompting me to say, "Ann, when we get home, I'm going to pull your tooth."

Her reply, "Daddy, are you a real doctor?"

I said, "No," but explained that I would be in a very few months.

To which she replied, "I want a real doctor to pull my tooth."

KID TALK

My kids had been bickering and teasing for a while and I, having had enough of this, told them that if they couldn't say something nice to each other, not to say anything. Consequently, son John said, "Ann, your acne is looking very nice."

There were two pieces of cake left at the end of dinner. Both Ann and John claimed them. John took the larger piece. Miss Manners, Ann, told John that if she had had first choice, she would have taken the smaller piece.

He said, "What are you kicking about. That's the piece you got."

WHAT A MESS!

When daughter Ann was married to Joe H., my cousin Ray and wife Sally came to the wedding. At the rehearsal dinner, champagne was served which got my Aunt Cora Lee Cox's attention. Her son Ray had informed her of this happening upon his return to Alabama, and knowing that the Marshes and Coxes were non-drinkers, she asked, "What did you all do?"

Ray replied, "We turned our glasses over."

My sweet second mother Cora Lee asked, "Didn't that make an awful mess?"

MIS-IDENTITY

Once when Judy and I were boarding an airplane, a youngster caught sight of me as I, cabin baggage in hand, came down the aisle. He was seated next to his father, and as we approached their seats, he excitedly pulled his father's arm, pointed at me and exclaimed, "Captain Kangaroo, Daddy, Captain Kangaroo."

As we passed by, he turned in his seat and continued to misidentify me to all who would listen as we moved toward our seats. The kid must be given, at least, some credit for seeing some resemblance as once when I was cutting through a parking lot in Gatlinburg, Tennessee, the attendant asked if I were Bob Keeshan. It's bad enough to be mistaken for Captain Kangaroo, but without the accompanying financial compensation, it's too much.

DAMN YANKEES

I had two very different grandfathers. My maternal grandfather, James P. Cox was born January 8, 1864 and died August 11, 1933. He died when I was about four years old, and I'm not completely sure I remember him. He was, by all accounts, a very poor, but honest, hardworking, and most of all, a kind man. During his last years, he was sick and his very last year, he was unable to make a crop. His and my grandmother's estate was $87.00 at his death. Death was due to Pellagra according to surviving family members.

My paternal grandfather was quite different. He was a Justice of the Peace and Mayor of Arab, Alabama, and I remember him well: an aloof, autocratic, impatient, do-it-my-way kind of man. He was born August 8, 1858 and died March 5, 1952. His wife, my grandmother, was a kind, considerate, cowed woman. Since my grandfather lived to be 94 years old, I was 23 years old when he died. However, that wasn't long enough to get even one hug, a pat on the head, or an ice-cream cone as a child and less, if possible, as an adult.

He did, however, tell the story of his father's, my great grandfather's, being an engineer on a Confederate railroad during the Civil War. As his account went, the train, to which my great grandfather was assigned, wrecked. The fireman jumped before the crash and was killed, but my great grandfather stayed with the engine and was neither killed, nor seriously hurt. However, word reached home that he had been killed, and it took him one month to get home after the wreck. While he was away, my great-grandmother had given birth, and when the child was but a few weeks old, and as my great grandmother lay in bed with "milk fever," a Yankee patrol came, consisting of a lieutenant and a squad or so of men.

There were no livestock except the milk cow, which the Yankees proceeded to take. They also laid claim to the sweet potatoes which were all there was to eat, taking only those that had no major rotten areas. They also looked for items of wealth, and as a means of search, they lifted my great grandmother by picking up the sheet upon which she lay and carrying her thus, placed her in the yard. The mattress was then torn apart revealing nothing of value and the house, ransacked. They did find corn, which was given to the soldiers' horses. According to my grandfather, the corn falling from the horses' mouths to the ground could be reclaimed, but the corn in the trough was not to be touched. My grandfather grabbed a handful from the trough in spite of swift and sure punishment by a rifle butt to the head – rough treatment, indeed, for a six or seven year old.

On the farm, there were but four people, my grandfather, his mother, his baby brother, and a Negro Mammy who pled for the retention of the cow as my grandmother had no milk for the baby. She made the point that taking the cow would be tantamount to killing the baby. Her pleas fell on deaf ears, and the soldiers left with the cow, corn, and sweet potatoes. Mammy, the heroine of this story, assigned my grandfather to picking out the least rotted potatoes that were pared of the rotten spots; he then picked up the corn on the ground, and also any uneaten corn remaining in the troughs. Mammy and my grandfather chewed very finely whatever food there was left, putting it in the baby's mouth sustaining him until my great grandfather arrived home sometime later.

This episode from his childhood left my grandpa Marsh with a very strong dislike for Yankees till the day he died. To him, Yankees were always *Damn Yankees*.

PATIENTS ARE WHERE THEY FIND YOU

I had an uncle who was, for many years, a GP and practiced, for the most part, in small hamlets and towns in Alabama. Once a patient asked him on the street for something for hemorrhoids. Uncle Stewart said, "Drop your pants and bend over." The patient demurred saying, "Right here on the street?" Uncle Stewart replied, "You asked me right here on the street."

SENTENCED BY JUDGE LAWRENCE

I have told you about my affection for my uncle Lawrence. Most of us, by nature, do not care for funerals, but if there is such a thing as a good funeral, it was his. There was some laughter, appropriate, of course, as the proper response to comments made by my uncle's pastor.

Rev. Absher told of visiting with Lawrence as he (Lawrence) did some work for the Arab, Alabama Baptist Church. The big news of the day concerned a jailbreak at Guntersville, the county seat. It seems that in the jailbreak, there was a gunfight with the High Sheriff having been killed during the escape and a deputy having been wounded. The pastor asked Lawrence what he thought about that. Lawrence said, as he wiped the sweat from his face that hot summer day, "I hope they catch them (the jail breakers), and if they're found guilty, sentence them to life, with their punishment being laying carpet in the attics of Baptist churches in Alabama in August."

A welcomed tension-relieving laugh swept through the audience.

THE MOST MEMORABLE ADVERTISEMENT I EVER SAW

Painted on the side of a brick building on Highway 29 between Auburn and Opelika, Alabama, "If the jerk in your car is other than the one sitting next to you, see us." Jamison's Auto Transmission.

Uncle Lucas Stories

The most profane man I ever knew was my Uncle Lucas. Uncle Lucas married my aunt Minnie, a sweet, kindly, and outgoing person with a good sense of humor. She was a widow who had two adolescent boys. It is a family story that Uncle Lucas hanged these two boys on the clothesline, but Aunt Minnie rescued them and resuscitated them before they expired.

Uncle Lucas was a bullet-headed man of medium build with closely cropped hair and a *five o'clock shadow*, as a heavy growth of hair just beneath the facial surface was known in those days. His bearded area was always dark causing a bluish-black discoloration of that area, and remember that we are talking about the days of straight razors and razor "strops," a leather strap wherein the razor was stroked to obtain the sharpest possible edge.

Talking Machine

As a consequence of his coarse and difficult to shave beard, he usually visited the barbershop three times a week for a shave. He often did not shave between these visits. On this particular day while seated in the barber chair, getting his shave, a drummer, old title for salesman, came in and began his pitch trying to sell "talking machines." The reader may have seen these in museums. They were wound up with a crank, played a very thick record and had what is commonly called a *tulip shaped speaker* – Victrola was the most popular brand of the day. The salesman, completing his sales pitch, addressed Uncle Lucas as a prospective purchaser and was surprised to hear Uncle Lucas say, "I already have a talking machine."

When the salesman asked, "What kind?" Uncle Lucas replied, "I married a damn Marsh."

On Following Directions

One day while plowing, with mule, of course, as tractors were so uncommon as to be a curiosity, Uncle Lucas was approached by a stranger asking directions. The stranger, driving a car, was told to turn around, proceed to a fork in the road, take the left fork, go about one-and-a-half miles to a crossroads, turn right and proceed about a half-mile to his desired destination. The recipient of the directions thanked Uncle Lucas saying, "I think I've got it, but kindly repeat the directions again." Uncle Lucas did so and upon the direction replay, the man again thanked Uncle Lucas. As the man turned to leave, but with his still being somewhat unsure, asked for the repetition of the directions once more. This time, Uncle Lucas said, "Turn around, proceed to the fork in the road, take the left fork, and go straight to Hell."

Gravely

While Uncle Lucas had a deserved reputation in the area for being obstreperous, with the ladies in his presence always keeping their backsides to the wall (he was a pincher), he did have one redeeming quality. When there was a death in the community, he could be counted on to dig the grave. Now, those were the days before backhoes, and the digging was with pick and shovel.

One very cold February day, he had been by mule and wagon twelve miles to Guntersville to get a casket. The trip back was characterized by a long, rather steep climb up Brindlee Mountain, and at the top of the climb there is a community named Grassy, complete in those days with country store and glowing pot-bellied stove. Uncle Lucas entered the store, stomping the snow off his shoes and relishing the thought of getting warm while allowing the mules to rest after their ordeal of climbing the mountain.

The store keeper knew him and exclaimed, "Mr. Prince, what in the world are you doing out on a day like this?"

Uncle Lucas replied, "I've been to Guntersville to get a casket for old man Mason."

The storekeeper replied innocently, but not too smartly, "Why, is he dead?"

To which Uncle Lucas replied testily, "Why the *blankety – blankety – blankety – blankety* hell do you think I would be out on a day like this, getting a casket for a live man?"

Marsh ancestors, adults (L to R) Glenn's great grandmother, Martha Ann Taylor Marsh (a niece of President Zachary Taylor) b. 2-24-1840 d. 10-4-1905; great-grandfather, Thomas Pemberton Marsh b. 6-27-1833 d. 1-17-1901; grandfather, William Pemberton Marsh, b.8-8-1858 d. 3-4-1952; grandmother, Emma Lenora Geiger Marsh b. 9-24-1862 d. 9-22-1946; boy standing is Glenn's father; infant in grandmother's lap is Glenn's Aunt Mamie. Thomas Pemberton Marsh is the great grandfather who was the engineer on the Confederate train which wrecked during the Battle of Atlanta. Picture circa late 1890s. Photo courtesy of Dr. Leon Marsh

PHILOSOPHY OF MEDICINE AND LIFE

GOLDEN AGE OF MEDICINE

I was fortunate to have practiced medicine in what I believe will be called "The Golden Age of Medicine," characterized by revolutionary developments in all branches of medicine and surgery, but before the intrusion by insurance companies and government into the day-to-day office and hospital practice. My colleagues still practicing remind me that I retired before the great change in medicine, the advent of HMO, PPO, POS days with physicians' having to get permission to admit patients to the hospital, with the length of stay being determined by insurance companies rather than by the doctor who knows the patient personally.

When I retired in 1989, I did not quite comprehend the significance of leaving the grand vocation of medicine, an entity that would be almost unrecognizable within a few years. C.S. Lewis notes that it is the nature of vocation to appear simultaneously as both desire and duty. "To follow the vocation does not mean happiness; but once it has been heard, there is no happiness for those who do not follow." Sometimes I think that instead of having heard clearly this "call" of vocation, in regard to many professions in today's world, it is more the sound of the bell at the close of the New York Stock Exchange, rather than the sound of the "muse" summoning one to the call of service. Gone are the days when patients chose their doctor(s) and to a certain degree, the doctors chose their patients, and neither was locked into a "bad marriage" of doctor/patient relationship. "Divorce," in this scenario, was simply changing doctors. Now, one must wait for *open enrollment* which occurs usually only once yearly to effect this change. I hear anecdotal stories of physician vs. physician fights over restrictive clauses, even though declared unethical by the AMA, and stories of fights over patients as well. I also see offensive ads in newspapers and on television touting members of the medical profession.

In company where I am not known as *Doctor*, I hear the complaints about doctors' being money hungry, non-caring, greedy, and so on and on. I do not like physician advertising and the same thing labeled as "public service" ads. I am glad I practiced medicine 1961–1989, and retired at the top of my game. Oh, we had some trouble, but the bad eggs were few and far between. I considered it an honor and pleasure to have referred to me, as patients, the children and the wives of colleagues, even if one surgeon sent his wife and all nine of his children over the years without one other referral.

In those days, it was practically unheard of for physicians, except psychiatrists, to charge other physicians or their wives or even their children prior to their reaching majority. Sadly, in the present medical climate, this gracious attitude, with both its supporters as well as its detractors among fellow physicians, has all but disappeared. I initially chose, as my family physician, one of my former students who had rotated through my office as a resident in Family Practice. I had excellent insurance that covered his charge except once I had a balance of $1.46. When I received his bill, I did not pay promptly, and before time for the second bill, we received a call from his office. A secretary reminded my wife of my oversight by saying, "Please ask Dr. Marsh to drop a check for the $1.46 by the office or put it in the mail as it is not *financially feasible* to send a reminder." I could not help but reflect that it had not been *financially feasible* for me to donate my time to instruct the Family Practice residents in dermatology, but then the practice of medicine should not be built primarily on the expectation of financial gain. While this experience is not unusual, my current family physician, also a former resident from Family Practice, reflects the gracious tradition that harkens back to my era. Thank you, Ritchie Van Bussum, for your dedication and adherence to the principles of a rapidly passing era. Often I extended this courtesy to nurses, nuns, ministers, irrespective of their faith, and the poor. "Money," as someone has said, "is a wonderful servant, but the worst of masters."

To summarize, if I had it to do again, I would have the same policy.

I also thought it wrong to charge a patient who was mistakenly referred to me for procedures or treatments outside my scope. I would thus advise the patient that he/she ought really to see a member of such and such specialty, write down two or three names of physicians in that specialty whom I'd be willing to see personally and send the patient on his/her way without charge.

MEMORY OR LACK THEREOF

My good memory has served me well throughout my life and has brought me out of a difficult situation time and time again. However, it is certainly less than perfect, as the following examples will illustrate.

On a medical school psychiatry exam there were but five questions. One question specified a one-word answer only (psychiatrists do not wish to be overworked by grading papers). I could not remember the word; however, I remembered the page number in the textbook and the two examples given there with the names of the notable persons used to illustrate the point. I entered the above information squeezing it in on the exam sheet and received sixteen points out of a possible twenty on this question. I am glad, in this case, that the professor was willing to read more than a *one*-word answer.

Early one morning, about eight o'clock, a very attractive young lady brought her charge, a somewhat unkempt, slightly confused, middle-aged lady to see me. I examined her, arrived at the diagnosis, and had the nurse call the young lady into the examining room. I explained the problem, told her that there was a new medication, only very recently on the market – much better than previously used medications, and that I had used it approximately half-dozen times with excellent results. She nodded assent, and I wrote the patient's name on the prescription blank, but got no further. I had forgotten the name of the medicine. I had a visual picture of the medication, its physical appearance including packaging and knew that it was a two-word name – but I could not remember the two words. There were no 24 hour pharmacies, nor was this medication in the reference books – too new. I told the truth as above, offering to phone in the prescription later, and to have it delivered to her within a short time. She, with her charge in tow, left the office in a huff telling the secretary, "What kind of doctor is this that can't remember the name of a medicine?"

– An honest one. Sometimes the truth does hurt the teller.

On another occasion, a patient of long standing told me that she was moving to Florida, and since her problem was chronic, she asked me if I knew a dermatologist in that area of Florida. I replied, "I sure do," having in the past had several occasions to refer to this well-known dermatologist. I then opened my mouth to say his name, but my memory failed me. I sat there several seconds, seeming like minutes, and finally said, "I'm sorry, I've drawn a blank;" this immediately followed by, "That's it – Dr. Harvey Blank!"

To this day, I'm not sure she truly believed that remarkable coincidence in word choice that brought the physician's name to mind.

JAMES BARD, MD
WORTHY OF THE NAME DOCTOR

Dr. James Bard was the dermatologist at the Lexington Clinic when I opened my practice in Lexington. I already knew him, our having met at professional meetings somewhere or other. I paid a call upon him once it was determined that I would definitely be moving to Lexington. He received me graciously and was most helpful in the establishment of my practice. Valuable tips about hospitals, office personnel, equipment, and dozens of other subjects, he gave without hesitation, and as I was to confirm later, supplied with total and absolute honesty. While we are good friends, our interests vary and our paths do not cross socially very frequently. The point I wish to convey is that I hold him in the highest personal esteem, as have the patients I have referred to him on numerous occasions. Never have I heard a single complaint about him from other colleagues or the patients so referred. We had a marvelous professional relationship over these many years, and it was good for me to have him take care of my patients during my absences. I have written but one letter to the editor of the *Lexington Herald Leader*, our local newspaper, in the thirty plus years of residency in Lexington. This was on the occasion of Dr. Bard's being elected President of the Lexington Clinic. My letter bore testimony to his leadership role in the community and was a personal tribute regarding his friendship and kindness. Regrettably, the letter was not chosen for publication. Perhaps, it was too personal, or not controversial. Should I ever list the reasons that make Lexington a desirable place to live and work, he and Elaine would be near the top of the list.

Sometimes, my patients resisted my attempts to refer them to another dermatologist – always Dr. Bard. Their almost uniform response was, "But I'm pleased with you. Why do you want me to see someone else?"

My reason as I would explain to them was, "My other patients with the same disorder have improved more than you

Dr. James and Elaine Bard of Lexington, Kentucky. Jim was the dermatologist and a former President of the Lexington Clinic. He is now retired and presently writing a history of the Lexington Clinic.

have by this time, and I am concerned that I am missing something."

While I was insistent on trying to help them, it sometimes took a summary and reassuring statement such as, "If the new doctor recommends continuing management as we have been doing, and doesn't find something else or doesn't disagree with my diagnosis, I'll be most happy and honored to have you return to my care anytime." This then worked out for all of us.

Dr. Bard's patients on seeing me when he was unavailable, on vacation, or because of his just wanting my input, I believe, never, ever wished to change to me. They were smart enough to know when they had the best. It was for this reason that when I retired, I chose not to sell my medical practice, but to give my patient records to Dr. James Bard and the Lexington Clinic because I felt that my patients deserved my loyalty, hence they should have the very best, Dr. James Bard at the Lexington Clinic.

BIRTH DEFECT

As I was nearing the end of my career as a dermatologist and phasing out my practice by not accepting new patients, there were some with chronic dermatologic illnesses that would need long-term care, so I suggested their follow-up be with Dr. Bard. Most understood readily, some asked me to reconsider retirement and a few cried. For those who could not pay, Dr. Bard was a Godsend as he assumed their care on those terms as I had done. I remember a few persistent patients who wanted to know more about him, my initial personal recommendation not being quite enough. For those, I spelled out a few of his numerous fine qualities. A very, very few of these patients wanted to know his shortcomings, if any. For this select group, I'd lean forward in my chair with an air of confidentiality and say, "Well, since you asked me, he has one fault of which I am aware."

The patient would ask in the same hushed tone, "What's that?"

My reply, "This fault is not now nearly so pronounced as when I first met him twenty-five years ago. His fault is a birth defect. He was born on the wrong side of the Ohio River. He's a *Damn Yankee.*"

With that, all resistance disappeared. We'd share a good laugh, and they'd make their appointment with Dr. Bard. Not too long after this little prank, Jim called to say, "I hear I have a birth defect." And I was able to share a laugh with him. A friendship like this is a rare and beautiful thing. We meet every few months for lunch and fellowship. Thank you, Jim.

TRIUMPH AND TRAGEDY

In my practice, I always felt that I did a decent job of being apprised of medical developments, and I did this by attending dermatology meetings and by reading the appropriate medical journals of my specialty. I had a patient of Italian descent, who having a plethora of skin tags, made visits over a few years for the removal of the most noticeable of these.

One day as I was reading my medical specialty journal, I read a study relating the increased incidence of internal malignancy in persons having these benign skin tags. As a result, I called him and made an appointment for him with an internist. His evaluation was negative, and I saw him about once a year for another two to three years until one day, he came without an appointment to inform me that he had a terminal malignancy.

I remember putting my arms around him, and we silently cried together sitting side by side on the examining table. Sometimes the best we can do is just not enough. Bart, I miss you.

During the writing of this manuscript, my Ohio daughter, Barbara M. called to check on me, and I told her that I had just finished the story on Bart. Did she remember him?

"Yes."

Did she remember his coming by the office in tears on his final visit?

"Yes!"

Then she asked me some questions about my memory concerning his death. As Barbara remembered, I was out west hunting and had checked in by phone when she told me of his death. I asked her to send flowers and to go to his funeral as my representative, which she did. I am so glad for this postscript to make the record complete.

On a happier note, sometimes things do work out in a marvelous way. A male patient came to me one day with a peculiar, but happily for me and for him, a recognizable cutaneous eruption. I recognized it as erythema annulare centrifigum, which can be a cutaneous manifestation of an internal malignancy, a cutaneous marker of internal disease, if you will. I called an excellent internist and sent him right over for a thorough workup.

At the conclusion of the workup, absolutely nothing amiss was found. I advised the patient to return if there were any more skin findings. About three months later, he returned with another episode of the same skin condition. I called the same internist, informing him. He did not relish putting the patient through the same battery of tests again, especially so soon. Having a good relationship with the internist, I prevailed, asking him to do it again as a favor to me. I just had a *feeling* that I was right.

Off the patient went with no small credit due him for his confidence in the medical profession, and lo and behold, this time, a digital exam revealed a small colon cancer; the lesion was removed surgically, and the bowel resected without necessity of colostomy.

I did not know the surgeon who operated, but in an act of personal kindness, he dropped by the office, telling my secretary that he wanted to meet the doctor who could diagnose colon cancer by looking at the patient's skin. I appreciated the praise of this surgeon very much. Admittedly, the above is a rare event, but what a great outcome for the patient.

I have always been an early starter. One reason is that I've never considered myself particularly bright and working harder, including getting an earlier start, allowed me to be competitive with those who were blessed with being brighter.

This trait carried over to the way my office was organized. I started patient appointments at 8:00 a.m. I know a few physicians who are doing that now, but as far as I know, I was the only one starting that early in 1968 when I began practice in Lexington. I also found that when I had patients in the hospital, if I went by to see them before 7:00 a.m., I could get the undivided attention of the nurses who were, at that hour, not sharing their time with a group of other doctors.

The downside to this happened one morning when I was in my office seeing the first patient of the day at 8:00 a.m. when there was a call, an emergency call, from an allergist's office in the same professional building. The allergist had not arrived when a patient sitting in his waiting room, with no warning quit breathing, while awaiting her appointment. I was summoned, left my patients, dashed up the one flight of stairs, and found a young lady in profound distress with pronounced cyanosis. With her doctor's staff for help and skilled cooperation, we injected appropriate medications, administered oxygen, and waited for an ambulance, which arrived promptly. The mother and I rode with the patient to the nearest hospital, about eight blocks away. When we arrived at the emergency room, a medical team, including an anesthesiologist, waited. The patient had spontaneously defecated and urinated, a most ominous event.

After intubation and other appropriate care, she was successfully resuscitated, and I returned to my office. Strange, but I don't remember who furnished the return transportation. By the time I arrived back at the office, most of the patients, upon hearing what had transpired, had wisely left, being reappointed, and one or two were miffed if not angry over their inconvenience.

The sister of the young lady transported to the hospital came by after a few days to thank me. The mother gave cursory thanks at the hospital, but I never heard from the patient, herself. Her doctor, the allergist, wrote me a very nice letter expressing his great appreciation. I did not render a bill considering the event a *Good Samaritan* act.

One day a man in his early fifties came in, referred by his family physician because of a pea-sized and shaped nodule on his scalp just above his left ear. It was asymptomatic, and his history was unremarkable except he had lost three to five pounds over the previous several months. His recent physical was entirely normal. After my exam, I sent my nurse, Sue, in to examine the lesion. She was an excellent nurse and student, albeit a bit of a mother hen with my being one of her chicks, along with her two children. I saw another patient, we then conferred, and when she asked me the diagnosis, I told her that it could well be a cutaneous metastasis from an internal malignancy. Being of appropriate inquisitive mind, she asked the likely source, and I rattled off in best residency rounds fashion, "breast, stomach, uterus, lung, intestine, and kidney," adding quickly that the patient being male, breast was unlikely, but possible, and uterus, of course, not a consideration. So I suggested stomach, most likely just by playing the odds. The lesion was removed, submitted to pathology, and in short order, I received a phone call from the dermatopathologist who complimented me on the correct diagnosis of metastatic stomach cancer.

I called the patient's family physician relaying the dreadful news. He agreed that he should be the one to tell the patient and further asked what I thought about treatment. Without hesitation, I used one word, "Palliative," the reasoning being that if his cancer had spread to the skin, it had spread elsewhere, especially in the abdominal cavity, which has no natural barrier. I further went on to say that while I knew nothing of the patient's financial status, it would appear that because of his relative youth, the man's estate needed to be conserved for his family, not be spent on oncologists, transfusions, and chemotherapy. His doctor agreed, and I had but one verbal follow-up a few months later when I learned that he was getting the complete battery of what we had thought not in his nor his family's best interest. I was so incensed at this, to me, a waste of the patient's estate, almost certainly to be needed by his wife, that I picked up a medical tome at random from my library and bounced it off the wall in a fit of anger, frustration, and exasperation directed toward my profession and colleagues. I don't ever remember being so angry and frustrated before or since. I finally cooled down and reconciled or rationalized my views with some probability that the family may have persuaded the responsible physician that, "If there were any chance at all, do something," and that maybe it was, after all, not clearly a situation of medical profession greed as first appeared. In writing this account, I still have an unhappy feeling about the whole management situation. The patient died less than six months after I met him.

BAD NEWS CAN WAIT, GOOD NEWS CANNOT

When I was a dermatology resident at Brooke Army Medical Center in San Antonio, Texas, I saw, upon referral, a female patient, wife of an Air Force enlisted man stationed in Hawaii. This couple had abruptly sold their home at a loss, disposed of their possessions, car, and furniture within a 72 to 96 hour period upon being advised that she had a melanoma involving her eye requiring enucleation, total removal of the eye. She had been told to be prepared for the worst.

Melanoma is a deadly malignancy that arises only in the pigmented areas of the body – three in number, skin, eye, and in a small part of the brain, the substantia nigra. The Ophthalmology Department at Brooke concurred in the diagnosis, but for some reason wished a dermatologic opinion, and I was assigned the consultation.

When I saw her, she was the epitome, along with her husband of abject, overwhelming anxiety. Having seen several melanomas previously, but none involving the eye, I proceeded to examine the lesion. I gathered a distinct impression that the problem was not a melanoma, but a benign cellular blue nevus, a kind of mole, which mimics a melanoma and is to be considered in the differential diagnosis. Having examined her thoroughly and having come to this conclusion, I, nonetheless, re-examined her, with the same strong clinical impression as before.

Now, what to do? I wanted to, as it were, shout to the housetops, that I disagreed with the diagnosis previously given, declare the good news, and in one fell swoop banish the dark pall of gloom surrounding this couple, and thus, put back together their now fragmented, disrupted lives. Instead, ever conscious of "pride goeth before a fall," I utilized again, the perfect teaching by the greatest Teacher of all, resolving to treat her as I would wish to be treated, not waiting another moment for the presumptive good news, I took her hand and in the calmest voice I could muster, told her that while I could be wrong, that

I disagreed with her previous examiners. I felt that the lesion was not malignant, but a benign mole, masquerading as a melanoma, further stating that a small biopsy of the lesion involving her iris would be diagnostic, and if I were correct in my diagnosis, no other treatment would be required. One can only imagine the response and the interaction between this wife and her husband. As I recall, I was in danger of losing my professional decorum also, so I excused myself, found the chief of dermatology and asked him to see the patient. His clinical impression was the same as mine. Biopsy fully confirmed our diagnosis: benign, cellular blue nevus.

Nobody's Perfect

I survived my more than two decades of private practice in Lexington with no brushes with the law, no malpractice suits, one threat, however, discussed elsewhere, and two complaints of misconduct to the grievance committee of the Fayette County Medical Society.

Since the first category is an empty one, and the second category is essentially the same as empty, we will delve into the third. I had a very large and very successful acne practice, which depended on a simple and direct approach. I had a basic regimen of three, usually office-supplied medications, as well as other prescription medications added as the need arose. These medications were available, not just at my office, but at the pharmacy in the adjacent professional building, as well as at another pharmacy in the city. The medications were effective, inexpensive, and the ingredients not a secret, as the formulae were freely given to any pharmacy requesting them. However, compounding was required, and only a very few pharmacists bothered to compound or stock the medications. An acne patient's mother, while pleased with her daughter's results, nonetheless, filed a complaint, claiming that the medications not being in every pharmacy in town, was somehow my fault, and that it was a burden for her to travel to those pharmacies that stocked the medications. The Society rejected this one out of hand.

The other complaint was that I required more return visits to effect a cure than formerly. This one reads like a fable: a father had two daughters about one to two years difference in their ages, and the first daughter had a plantar wart which was treated on the initial visit with the old standby, 40% Salicylic acid pad, "Don't get it wet, return in two weeks." Upon return when the pad was removed, out came the wart. Good!

About one to two years later, daughter number two had the same problem. Treated the same identical way, the wart, i.e. some residual wart remained at the end of the two weeks. Reapplication of the same medicine effectively removed the remainder of the wart. Bad! Doc is requiring a third visit now. He should have gotten rid of it in two visits like the first one, i.e. he's gilding the lily with an extra-visit, extra-charge routine. My reply to the grievance committee was short and sweet: "Kindly name any practitioner of any medical specialty who wouldn't settle for the removal of a typical plantar wart in three visits. They agreed.

"Horse Feathers"

In this same realm, I also averted a potential problem by being informed in matters where the world of medicine meets the world of law.

After I had been in practice for about three years, I received a call from a prominent horseman, asking that I make a trip to his farm, examine, and treat one of his most expensive horses having a skin condition. I had arrived, or had I? I remembered the orthopedist in Florida, who was sued by veterinarians when he did surgery on a horse without having a degree in veterinary medicine, or a license to practice it. After this sobering thought, I decided to "make my mark" caring for patients who walk on two legs.

In summing up the state of affairs in regard to our contemporary, litigious society, a black expression from my growing up years in Alabama comes to mind: "We'se passin' up more'n we'se catchin' up with."

AGGRAVATION

Church folks, especially in my own church, were the hardest to please, most demanding patients, I experienced. On one occasion after several unnecessary calls, always at home and always late at night, I reminded the patient firmly, but not unkindly, that he was not the only patient I had. There were several instances of church or attempted church consultations, and I should have done as the lawyer in our church did; bill these folks. He did that, I think, only once; the word got around quickly, and that practice stopped. I wasn't nearly so smart and one Wednesday night at prayer service, the wife of the family (as she had repeatedly done before), dragged her child before me in inadequate light, in the midst of people, and wanted me to render an examination and a medical opinion. I am sorry to say that I said pointedly, "I've seen patients all day at the office, and I am not going to have a Baptist Church clinic on Wednesday nights." More than she heard it, and that was the last of it, except the offender was quite offended. I handled that very badly. Some parishioners had actually suggested that I render treatments at church.

USING PRECISE LANGUAGE

Mark Twain is quoted as saying that, in writing or speaking, one must use the one correct word as befits the occasion. An almost correct word will not do. It must be correct. He used the analogy of the difference between the word "lightning" and "lightning bug." Good for you, Mr. Clemens, but it "don't" necessarily work in medicine. I'll never forget when instead of using the common term "fever blister" referring to the lesion on the teenager's lip, I inadvertently used the medical term "herpes labialis" in the presence of the patient and her judgmental mother.

This precipitated an emotional storm. Older said, "You did." Younger said, "I did not."

I finally got them in neutral corners, but I don't think Mother changed her already-arrived-at opinion one bit. My conclusion: Don't use the precise word in every instance. In some situations, *horsefly* is better than *horse.*

NEARLY GETTING STUCK

When I began my internship of one year, I had two months of elective rotation. Since I had an idea of becoming an anesthesiologist, this was a natural choice, and since most people, at one time or another, will have a skin problem, I also chose a rotation in dermatology.

I really liked my anesthesia rotation and became adept at axillary blocks to the degree that my services were requested by some of the surgeons. Since one can tell a surgeon, but not much, I considered this a high accolade being a mere intern and being depended upon by the surgeon for anesthesia for a patient.

On this particular day I, along with a surgery resident, T. R. T., and the anesthesia resident, I.R., were in the operating room. The patient having surgery, also present, was to have epidural anesthesia. All three physicians were sterile gloved; with spinal needle inserted by the anesthesia resident when somehow the two residents bumped breaking the sterile field. Dr. I.R. told me to inject the medication in the syringe. I protested in that it was he, not I, who had positioned the needle. I, thus, felt uncomfortable injecting this medication. He exploded at this with, "You're just a damn intern. Do as I tell you!"

However, I had the last word saying, "I do this under protest."

I had no sooner injected the medicine than the patient's eyes rolled back, he could not speak or breathe. A TOTAL SPINAL. We intubated him, and I breathed for him via an air bag all afternoon until he was able, finally, to breathe on his own.

A short time after the initial incident, someone in the surgery lounge asked, "What's holding up OR # 3?"

My friend (?) the anesthesia resident replied, "The damn intern gave a total spinal." The surgeon present during the above happily rose to the occasion saying, "He did, but YOU positioned the needle and YOU demanded that he inject which he did with protest."

Moral of the story: hero and goat are but one step apart. Also, not everyone with MD behind his/her name is honorable.

ACNE

One of my real challenges in acne management came about because I had seen a U.K. coed with this problem, and she was from extreme western Kentucky, not far from Memphis, where a dermatologist had seen her brother. She had done very well, indeed, and showed her new complexion at home. Her father brought, by his private plane, her brother who had the oiliest face I had ever seen. I cannot describe how terribly oily this young man was. Undaunted, I predicted, not promised [there's a big legal difference here] improvement upon his return visit in two weeks, same as any other patient. Upon return, he was not improved and of course, still oily. I dug deep into my "get 'em dry" bag of tricks, added another medication and asked that he return in a month.

When he returned, he was not as oily, but not nearly as improved as expected. In desperation, I added a medication not having been necessary ever before or since and upon the patient's return in one month – success! Skin was dry, practically no new lesions, and what was then needed was a maintenance program as a cure is unknown, and the patient was dismissed. Not once did the father complain about the cross state flights. Four visits for severe acne before Acutane days was about average.

What miracle medications did I use? None. My program was primarily geared to removing oil from where it was excessive and this done repeatedly during the day where increased activity both mental and physical seemed to stimulate it. I used also a nighttime drying medication, which was formulated to offer some resistance to washing off in the morning, which resulted in some light scrubbing, which resulted in efficient removal of the oil. Of course, I used Tetracycline or Minocycline, but never thought these medicines as important as the oil removal approach. The theory was that the antibiotics eradicated the nonpathogenic organisms normally present on the skin involved in the acne process, by converting the skin oils into irritating fatty acids, which caused the acne lesions themselves. How much scientific validity exists for this theory, I don't know, but my simple approach helped many people. Makeup caused my program to jump the tracks, so to speak, so I had a hard sell trying to keep the fairer sex away from makeup. Obviously, that being the case, my results were better or at least less difficult in achieving in males.

I have heard more than one dermatologist say, "Some days I believe that if I have to see one more acne patient, I'll . . . ."

I have never felt that way because for one thing, I enjoyed very much being a doctor to this age group. I liked seeing their response, often going from withdrawn to outgoing in a very few weeks as they responded to treatment. I liked the exuberance of youth and felt younger myself at the end of the day at the office, as most acne patients were seen from three p.m. till closing time. It was always a nice way to end the day.

I liked developing their confidence and trust on the first visit, setting realistic goals, and sharing their joy upon achieving these goals. We would then build upon the stepping-stone goals until the patient was ready for dismissal. I always complimented the patient telling him/her that the improvement was a direct result of his/her action while I had the easy job of only telling how and when and what to do. Placing the responsibility on the patient in this age group reaped great dividends as the kids took responsibility not only for improving to what I called MOB, maximum office benefit, but crucially important, they maintained the program when dismissed by continuing this responsibility they had learned; therefore, I was never known as a "Come-back Dermatologist." This also fostered a good relationship with the bill-paying parents. Did all the acne patients comply? Of course not, but I had outstanding success as this group made up a large part of my patient census.

For those patients who did not improve because of noncompliance, I would have what I called a "bare knuckles conversation," and I was quite frank and pointed; if the patient simply did not really wish to improve or was not willing to be responsible and was evidently not following or only haphazardly following the program, I would tell the teenager that I was not going to be his/her accomplice in ripping off the parents. "If you are not going to follow the program, OK. Just say so. On the other hand, whenever you want to get serious, I'll be here to help." Not a few, over the years, would return in a few months, attitude changed and ready to be responsible.

It always concerned me that most dermatologists did not seem to be bothered by the excessive oiliness of the acne prone areas or believe the statement, "Not everyone who has oily skin has acne, but everyone who has acne, has oily skin." Like all truisms, this is not always true. For example, certain medications, such as steroids, and certain diseases, hyperthyroidism, for instance, can be associated with acne. I once saw a new patient, aged 40-plus, with acne and when shaking hands, noticed his moist, warm palm. So I took his pulse, which was quite elevated as well as his blood pressure. Laboratory studies revealed that he was in "thyroid storm." One never knows what other pathology the acne patient might have.

On another occasion, I saw a teenager (P. P.) in the wintertime for acne and even though wearing a winter coat, I noted that she had very broad shoulders and much narrower hips than would have been expected. As a result of this, an examination revealed that she did, indeed, have a very muscular configuration of the body, so much so that her mother related that she would not wear dresses, only slacks. A biopsy revealed that she had no subcutaneous fat at all. As a result of the complete workup, she was found to have lipo-atrophic diabetes, a most uncommon, even rare condition. This particular diabetic state is insulin resistant, and I suppose, the patient is no longer living. An internist and I collaborated in writing a paper on this patient, which was subsequently published.

Not everyone who has acne has just acne.

THE RIGHT MIX

People used to ask me, "What does it take to be a good dermatologist?"

I would reply, "Not much, look at me."

I think the most important thing is to have a good memory. One must see a case, or even read about it and be able to call it up from memory, be a keen observer with good vision to see the minute features of the disease process, have an inquisitive mind so as to develop a good medical history to arrive at the etiology, and have acquired enough knowledge of internal medicine and pediatrics, to relate the skin findings as a possible manifestation of a systemic disease.

SMALL WORLD #3

My father was a carpenter, who, before and after WW II, built houses. His house-building was interrupted because of WW II, as building materials for this purpose were not available. Those were the days of digging footings with pick and shovel, mixing concrete on the site, and plastering the walls and ceilings with real plaster, not drywall.

One of the most brilliant members of the faculty at Auburn, Dr. Fred Allison, approached my father about hiring his son Fred. My father told this learned man that the only job he had open was day labor, i.e. pick and shovel work. The professor said, "Exactly what I have in mind. My son Fred needs to be toughened up; he's soft."

The next day Fred Jr. reported to work on time, 7:30 a. m., in the hot Alabama summertime. He was wearing a white dress shirt, perhaps, no longer good enough to qualify for a tie, decent slacks and shoes, and no hat and no gloves. Before long, there was a tear in the shirt, more tears, and then no shirt at all as it was discarded. The sweat poured as the skin reddened and at the end of the day, Fred Jr. looked decidedly bad.

My dad whispered to me, "Fred Jr. won't be here tomorrow."

I should digress and say that I sure did like going to work with my father in those days. I liked being with him. I didn't have much to do. I was too little to really work, so I'd take books, a Hardy Boy book if I could borrow one, and if not, I'd whittle.

I didn't have a good knife, so I'd borrow my daddy's with a stern accompanying admonition, "Don't lose it!"

Also, if things went really well for me – not Daddy – he'd have to go to the lumberyard or building supply, and usually that meant a stop at the Gulf filling station located at the northeast corner of N. College and Tichenor Avenue for a "Co-Cola" for him and a Nehi orange or grape drink (10 ounce vs. six-and-one-half ounces) for me. Mr. Leroy Harrison was the proprietor, succeeded in later years by Mr. Robert Ingram.

My daddy was seldom wrong, but he was this time. When we pulled up at the building site early the next morning, Fred Jr. was there waiting. Daddy was direct, "Fred, I didn't expect you to be here today."

Fred said, "I didn't sleep too good last night with my sunburn, and I couldn't get my hands to work this morning. I turned on the water faucet with my elbows and ran hot water on them for a while to get them to work. So here I am."

This made a profound impression on my dad, and while he already had a strong respect for Fred's father, Dr. Allison, Fred Jr. now had also gained his respect.

My father told this story for years and now I have "the rest of the story."

When I was the dermatologist at Fort Knox and chief of hospital clinics there, I was responsible for separation of military personnel from the service for a variety of reasons, most were recent draftees who by Army regulation had conditions that disqualified them from Army service. Remember the old joke about Army doctors each of whom looked into a patient's ear simultaneously, and if they didn't see each other, the person was fit for military service.

I saw in the Dermatology Clinic such a patient with a rare congenital disease that in time would lead to blindness, heart disorders, and early death. He was from Mississippi, and I made a note of his name and address. A year or two later the Southeastern Dermatology Society was to meet in Jackson, Mississippi so looking at a map, I decided that if this former patient now discharged from the Army would or could come to the meeting, that he would be an ideal patient for presentation and discussion. I corresponded with him and he agreed to come. The clinical part of the program was held at the University of Mississippi Medical School Hospital, and while there, as I was walking down the hall to present this patient at our clinical conference, I saw a medical school professor who looked like, yes, it was Fred Jr. He was glad to see me and laughed again at his toughening up experience under the tutelage and at the hands of my father.

Mention of the presentation of this patient reminds me of another occasion at Fort Knox, when I saw a draftee who was referred to me for an evaluation of a blood vessel tumor of his leg. When he stood facing me, he was a human "Leaning Tower of Pisa." He tilted at about fifteen degrees. When examined, he had a massive, cavernous hemangioma resulting in more blood supply to the leg bones on that side with subsequent overgrowth causing the leg on the affected side to be much longer. Of course, I discharged him. He should never have been inducted and only the sloppiest physical exam would miss this obvious problem. It did remind me, however, of the old Army doctor story.

DUTCH TREAT

I had not been in practice long in Lexington when this well-known gentleman came to see me. I did not know until later that he was a manufacturer of, at least, local renown with his products being common in the larger food stores. He had a moderately severe eczema and as usual was placed on appropriate medication, and I asked that he return in two weeks for a follow-up.

He returned as scheduled, much improved, but not completely clear, so I made some changes from the first medication to a safer medication for long-time use as needed and dismissed him from my care unless a recurrence [which was likely] could not be reversed by the first medication which he was to keep on hand.

When he left the office on his follow-up visit, he balked at paying the $5 return visit fee. My secretary, who had fielded his complaint, advised that his position was that since he had improved so much, he shouldn't have been asked to return.

I wrote him a nice letter thanking him for his choosing me and explaining that office overhead required a charge. I further stated that it would be nice if I were independently wealthy so that I would not have to charge. However, since I was not, a charge was indicated. I went on to say in the letter that if his financial situation was such that he could not pay, to please sign his name at the bottom of the letter, return the letter to me, and his account would be satisfied.

In a few days, I received a check for $5. He really was Dutch, though now, many, many years later, deceased Dutch.

House Calls

I don't personally know any doctors who now do house calls. I did house calls and found them professionally satisfying, but inefficient, although, I never thought being efficient was a parameter of good medicine.

On one occasion, I did a house call about thirty-five miles away, calling on this little old lady who was curved by arthritis into a capital C configuration. When she sat in the chair, I kneeled in front of her to make eye contact. It was evident that she could not get into an automobile and ride therein. I found her to be a delightful patient and her whole family was grateful.

Her family consisted of four middle aged, unmarried daughters. During my years in practice, she, together with all of her family, except one daughter, died. All were loyal patients.

Similar to a house call, but not quite the same, was my calling on those at the local Catholic facility for the elderly. I was especially well received by these folks and enjoyed visiting with the patients and the nuns.

Don't Quit

A retired dentist came upon appointment to see me one day. As he had had an office in the professional building next door until he retired, I had previously met him, but was unprepared for his outburst when I greeted him, "Hello, Dr. Dennis. How are you?"

He nearly yelled the word, "Terrible!"

I was taken aback, and recovering said, "What in the world is the problem?"

Continuing in a loud voice he said, "The first mistake I made was retiring; the second mistake I made was selling my farm; the third mistake I made was moving into a condo. Now, I don't have a thing to do, not a blade of grass to cut – nothing."

I said, "Well, Doctor, how do you spend your time?"

His answer floored me, "I take out groceries at the A & P Food Store."

This most unhappy man could have made a great hospital volunteer, working where his background and knowledge could have been beneficial. He felt unneeded, useless, and worthless.

I read his name in the obituary section of the local paper less than six months later.

How sad!

RETIREMENT

When my twenty-year lease at Medical Heights expired in 1989, I decided to retire. I did give thought to staying on another two or three years, but the time had come to quit. Many patients were incredulous that I would retire so soon, knowing how I loved my vocation. Others said, "You won't stay retired. You love it too well." My friend and colleague Jim Bard, MD offered me a position at the Lexington Clinic shortly after my

Glenn and Judy Marsh in medical office, 2368 Nicholasville Road, Lexington, Kentucky, shortly before retirement in 1989

retirement, but I declined. What a professional treat it would have been to practice with him, with whom I had so much in common, but the answer was still a respectful no.

Accolades from my patients brought the most in psychic income. I often thought and sometimes said, "How else can one enjoy themselves so much and even be paid for it?" At this writing, twelve years retired, I'm still getting a few calls for appointments, and just yesterday one of the staff at the appointment desk at the medical office where I was making a return appointment told me that she had mentioned to her mother that she had recently met me. Her mother, who had been one of my patients, had nice things to say about me to her daughter and remembered I was something of a cutup or tease. This is not an uncommon occurrence as I find myself, these days, on "the other side of the waiting room," oft times sitting beside or across from a former patient with whom I can reminisce. The psychic income continues.

Judy and I have written three papers presented at the American Society of Arms Collectors. Judy is an accomplished photographer and that helps immensely. Her layout advice going back to when she was in charge of the Bardstown High yearbook is invaluable. The first paper, given in Cincinnati was entitled *Benjamin Mills: Outstanding Kentucky Gunmaker of the Nineteenth Century*; and the second, a companion paper, given in Richmond, Virginia, was *John Madole: Outstanding Kentucky Gunmaker of the Twentieth Century*. The third paper, given in Charleston, South Carolina was *Identifying a Kentucky Longrifle: The George Schreyer, John Fondersmith, JFS Connection*.

As students of the Oregon Trail, Judy and I have retraced the trail from Independence, Missouri all the way to Oregon once, and on four other treks, we have studied various segments of the trail starting in Missouri, going through Kansas, Nebraska, and concluding in Wyoming and Idaho, even flying over parts of it in a private plane so as to view the ruts from the air. In this endeavor, we have met some interesting and fine

Judy and Glenn at an American Society of Arms Collectors meeting where we have given three papers. circa 1990s. Dan Schlegel in background (friend and fellow Kentuckian who is also a member of the ASAC.)

people, especially in Wyoming. The Barbers in Wyoming have their own private exit from the interstate highway, with this exit going *only* to their ranch. The Oregon Trail goes right through their property where there's a trailside grave with the ruts of the wagons quite visible. On one of our trips, the Barbers graciously invited us to go with them on a special trek planned and guided by Mr. Randy Brown over Rocky Ridge, a very rugged, nearly impassable part of the trail. What gracious folks they are.

Other westerners, whom we admire, are the Bucks. Now, however, just Karen survives. She and her mother remain sleuths of the trail. Both have made significant findings and contributions to the fund of knowledge on this subject. Karen has 36 square miles of ranch through which the trail passes, and with their altitude, they have only 18 frost-free mornings per year. Needless to say, rhubarb thrives there.

Our first meeting with Karen and her family was an interesting one. We found her name in several places in our literature

Glenn and Judy, South Pass, Wyoming on the Oregon Trail beside a marker placed there in 1906. There are pristine wagon ruts visible. Photo circa 1998

Karen Buck, her mother Alice Antilla, and Glenn, circa 1999. Mrs. Antilla was one of the earliest sleuths of the Oregon Trail. Karen has made many interesting trail discoveries and was a wonderful guide during the trip on the Sublette Cutoff segment of the trail. A good friend is she.

on the Oregon Trail, and contacted her by phone after a friend located her number via the Internet. Karen, who is an authority on the Sublette Cutoff of the Oregon Trail, agreed to take us through this part of the trail, a rugged desert. Even today, one does not go into this area alone. Karen, along with her second husband, met these two strangers from Kentucky on the roadside at the "False parting of the Ways" historical marker, provided us with a CB radio to communicate with them, and the caravan of two four-wheel-drive vehicles set off on the Sublette Cutoff. We traveled all day through the Little Colorado Desert, seeing only one other vehicle. Late in the afternoon, Judy and I questioned, "Where are we going to spend the night?"

Karen's answer, "At the ranch." What *southern* hospitality! I believe, perhaps, the westerners actually invented what we call southern hospitality.

A further interesting aspect of our meeting Karen occurred at the evening meal at the ranch. In discussing the various Oregon Trail historians, I happened to mention Alice Antilla, a trail historian from the very earliest days, stating, "I sure wish I could have met Alice Antilla. I'm sure she is probably dead by now, but she was one of the first trail historians about whom I have read."

Karen's next statement was a shocker, "Would you still like to meet her? She's my mother."

And so we did. What a treat! Both Karen and Mrs. Antilla remain our good friends.

A second bit of irony in regard to Karen occurred when Judy and I were taking our niece, Martha, to tour Wickland, Home of Three Governors, in Bardstown, Kentucky. Mrs. Sarah Trigg (the proprietor of Wickland and longstanding friend of both Judy and me) and I were chatting about the Oregon Trail while Judy and Martha were admiring the marvelous antique furnishings. I was telling Mrs. Trigg about Karen and our meeting her when Mrs. Trigg mentioned that the copy of *National Geographic* on the table between us had a marvelous article on the Oregon Trail. Picking up the magazine, I turned to the article and lo and behold, there was a picture of none other than – Karen Buck.

A second hard-to-believe incident also occurred in Wyoming on one of our retracings of the trail. As we were waiting to check into a motel in Torrington, we struck up a conversation with two middle-aged ladies also waiting to check in. Imagine our surprise when two days later we stopped at a roadside historical marker and there they were. I would like to know the mathematical odds on the probability of this happening.

On still another of the treks, we were looking for California Hill (which was then privately owned) in order to see the reportedly vivid ruts. Looking for the owner of the property to get permission to see the ruts, we were driving on an unimproved road which had the warning "Travel at your own risk," posted. On this stretch of road, we met a car with Virginia license plates. They stopped, we stopped, and meeting in the middle of the dirt road, I asked the gentleman if he knew the owner of California Hill and if he were, by chance, an Oregon Trail buff?

The term "buff" seemed to give him a bit of a problem. The reason being that he was from Denmark. He had brought his family to the United States, rented the car in Virginia, and set out west to – what else – retrace the Oregon Trail.

EDUCATIONAL BACKGROUND

All of my retirement has not been spent in traveling, nor did I intend it to be. A year or so after my retirement, I set about achieving a long-standing goal. I wanted to become competent in machine technology, i.e. lathe, milling machine, and other machine tools. Kentucky Vo Tech in Lexington offered such course work, and I went down to register. The lady in admissions asked me if I had a GED or equivalent, and I said, "Yes, ma'am," with no other comment. I paid my registration and course fee, bought my books, but before classes began, Judy learned that she would require surgery and would miss a large part of a semester of teaching. This, plus the fact that my back problems would likely preclude the ability to stand for long periods of time in shop, brought about my decision to withdraw even before classes began. No reason was required for withdrawing, and I gave none. However, when I came home after this administrative procedure, Judy teased me saying, "I'll bet one of those ladies said to the other, 'I'm not surprised he withdrew; anyone could look at him and tell that he didn't have a GED.'" In all fairness, my wife's comment stemmed from her observation of my manner of dress when going to apply for admission – I was comfortably robed in my choice, faded farm clothes with frayed collar and cuffs.

SHERIFF ANDY TAYLOR AND MISS CRUMP

Several years ago wife, Judy, and I had occasion to visit the hamlet in northern Indiana where she was employed for one year for her first teaching job. How the town had changed! No longer was there a local school. Consolidation, you see – and now the former school building was being used for storage for machine parts and showed marked neglect.

We noted that the downtown area had several boarded up businesses as we went to the offices of the lumberyard where former friends and acquaintances came to say hello and reminisce.

I was impressed that in just one year Judy had left her mark among school students, cooks, and office staff. Most remarkably near the end of the day, the sheriff came by, regrettably not accompanied by a Barney Fife, just the Sheriff with pants' cuff caught in boot top just like Sheriff Andy Taylor. He was a handsome man, and I took an immediate liking to him even though he had been Judy Love's [Miss Crump's] beau during that year. I found myself admiring his taste, but glad that the old doctor had won out over the young sheriff.

A sad footnote: so many of the people who came by timed the decline of the town to the loss of their own school. I believe they're right.

Glenn with granddaughter Mandy (age 16) 1994. Use of photo by permission of Tom Barnett Photography.

FAVORITE PROFESSORS

Since I noted in an earlier section, that Miss Lucille Rhodes was my favorite teacher from my pre-college days, I should take the opportunity to give tribute to the three very best professors of my post-secondary educational career. They are Dr. B. B. Williams, Professor Genady Michailovic Kosolopoff, and Dr. Marian Hines.

DR. B. B. WILLIAMS

Dr. B. B. Williams was my major professor for my Master's Degree in Pharmacology at Auburn. He was not on the faculty when I earned my Bachelor of Science Degree in 1950.

Dr. Williams was a brilliant teacher and a favorite of the students. He was free of pettiness and as fair as any teacher could be. His lectures were prepared so well that he never used or needed notes. His even temper and facility for grasping the nature of a problem were great assets. Maintaining a strong interest in my graduate studies at Emory University, he followed my course upon graduation from medical school. He and Mrs. Williams (Mary) even visited us in our sub-standard housing during student days in Atlanta where he attended lectures with me one day during medical school. I managed to keep in touch reasonably well over the years until his death a few years ago.

Byron Williams, PhD; wife, Mary Williams, and Glenn. Byron was one of my three favorite/best professors and my Major Professor for my Master's Degree at Auburn, 1955. Photo circa mid 1990s

PROFESSOR GENNADY MICHAEL KOSOLAPOFF

My second professor given the "Glenn Marsh Award" for best professor was Professor Gennady Michael Kosolapoff. Professor Kosolapoff was professor of organic chemistry at Auburn with his specialty being organic phosphorus chemistry. I had heard for years about teachers who wrote on the blackboard with one hand and who erased concomitantly with the other. He is the first and only one I ever knew who routinely did that. He also used no notes and when the lecture hour ended, he stopped precisely at that point, and the next lecture two days later began at precisely that same point. His favorite phrase, at least for those of us just getting into this discipline, was, "At this stage of the game."

I was surprised, years later, to learn from his son that at the time he was teaching at Auburn, he received financial support from our government (CIA) to monitor the development and state of production of organic phosphorus compounds by the Soviet Union.

Dr. Marian Hines

Dr. Marian Hines was professor of Neuroanatomy at Emory University, and was the third one of my three all-time favorite professors. In this assessment, personality plays no part. My evaluation is based exclusively on teaching ability, nothing else.

Dr. Hines' lectures in medical school were Monday, Wednesday, and Friday with Neuroanatomy lab on Tuesday and Thursday afternoons. Prior to her lectures, she would spend an untold amount of time on the drawings on the blackboard in the lecture room using colored chalk to fully illustrate her lectures. The lectures were timed perfectly and she did not tolerate distractions. On the third lecture of the course, a student, and I still remember his name – R. Y., interrupted her to ask a question. Her reply, "Mr. Y., I covered this material in the lecture on Wednesday, went over it again in lab yesterday. I don't cover the same material three times for anyone." There were no more questions interrupting her lecture the rest of the course.

I thought it remarkable that by the third lecture, she knew everyone of the students by name, and probably, this student was known for making himself known. There was an interruption of her class once more, this time by Dooley, the Emory mascot who by tradition, if he comes to a class, the professor was expected to dismiss the class. Dr. Hines' response to Dooley was two words, "Get out." He got.

There was but one exam, the final. No second chance here, but as an upperclassman told me, "Study daily, keep up, and at the end of the course, all will come together and be understood." He further said, "It will be like the sun coming up in the morning."

I followed this suggestion and while hard, the final was fair, and a proper assessment of what we had learned, or hadn't learned was revealed by the questions on the exam. I never saw

Dr. Hines again after that course, and she may or may not have welcomed a return visit by a student. I simply felt that I was in the presence of a great teacher and respected her ability.

OFFICE TOMFOOLERY

"*Tomfoolishment*" IN THE OFFICE

One April Fools' day as the morning progressed, I seemed to be getting further and further behind in seeing the scheduled patients. It was nearing 11:30 a.m. and I saw a stack of patient charts representing those still to be seen. I had been in my "hurry" mode for quite a while without apparent results. Then I happened to look out into the waiting room, and there was but one person waiting. This prompted my looking through the supposed patient charts of those yet to be seen. I discovered that they were all fakes. I'd been had. I congratulated the girls on their little joke, took them to lunch, and vowed silently that the next year, the laugh would be on them.

During the following year, my son, David, borrowed the family car to go on a date as he had done many times, but on this occasion when he went out to the car after he had taken his date home, there was a dirty diaper draped over the steering wheel. In disgust, he gingerly picked it up with great care by the corner, and as he prepared to dispose of it, noticed, with great surprise, that it had no odor. It was a fake, a very good fake, an excellent fake. He brought it home, and over a few days, we all marveled at its authentic appearance. It was soon rolled up, forgotten, and placed on a bookshelf near David's bed. Somehow it fell behind the bed and Beatrice, the maid, found it while house cleaning, came down the stairs in a snit saying, "What kind of folks is you? I been cleaning houses for years, and I ain't seen nothin' this nasty befo' in nobody's house!" I told her it was a fake, and she had a laugh when she heard about how we had come to have it.

Beatrice absent-mindedly left it on the counter in the kitchen and son John happened to drop by. He spotted it immediately, exclaiming angrily, "Daddy, you've got to talk to Ann [his sister] about leaving Mandy's [infant daughter of Ann] dirty diapers lying around, and began making his way to the back door outside of which was the garbage can, all the while holding the offending diaper by the tiniest grip on the corner. He also had to be informed as to the true nature of this new, wonderful item of fakery. With this, I knew that I had my April Fools' trick for the annual office who-gets-whom event.

In due time, April first rolled around and I heard one of the staff say to another, "Be alert, it's getting near the end of the morning, and nothing's happened yet, but it will." How right she was.

Finally, the morning schedule of patients had been seen, but I didn't yet have a plan as to how to use the masterpiece of fakery. Then it came to me. Now, I don't use profanity, never have, but on this occasion, decided it was needed for the complete surprise, as that would certainly surprise them. Now, Sue, my nurse, was always impeccably dressed for duty. Her nurse's uniform was so starched she rattled when she walked. Obviously, she'd be the target. I took the now-famous item by the equally famous corner, where else, held it out before me and marched up to the secretary's office where all were gathered. I walked up to them holding the item extended before me, so all could see, glowered at them and said angrily, "Now, you all know that I love a joke as much or more than anyone you know, but whoever put this dirty diaper on my desk has gone too damn far!" Shock was on their faces, accentuated by my convincingly angry countenance, punctuated by the "damn." I then planted the diaper, business-side toward the victim, at the base of Sue's neck. Sue broke into tears, and Barbara laughed after a short delay, saying that she knew immediately that I'd never do anything like that if it were not a joke. Sue recovered when the hoax was discovered, forgave me, and years after I retired, was the scrub nurse when I had cataract surgery.

Yes, I went too far.

The time I really, really went too far concerned a Halloween prank. Son John had a gruesome, but believable full face mask that, when tucked underneath the collar, was completely believable. He also had a full-length raccoon coat. Perfect! I left for work early that day, parking on the opposite side of the building whence the staff arrived. I threw the master electric switch in my office suite, and in my costume, sat in the dark waiting room to await their morning entry. The staff entered by way of the rear entrance. One came in and flipped the light switch several times with no results; soon another came in and went through the same routine. Then the two compared notes saying, "We'll put on the coffee and wait for him (Dr. Marsh)." The other said, "We can't make coffee without electric."

The other, "You're right."

I allowed them to settle down, silently arose, opened the door from the waiting room leading to the examining rooms, and stood there in the early morning gloom. I remained mute, and they were even "muter," gasping, trying to scream with vocal cords that would not work. In the meantime, they were stepping backward, ever backward. I was afraid too – afraid to move for fear they would have a heart attack.

The tension abated when Pat said, "Dr. Marsh, I recognize your shoes."

We all shared a shaky laugh. I admit, I was as scared as they were. Went too far again, but that wasn't the end of the terror. They wanted in on it, and even as the last patient of the morning was still in the office, I had turned off the lights in an examining room, hunkered down in the patient's dressing cubical in Halloween costume and awaited the response to the girls' telling the Family Practice resident that I had an emergency in that particular room. With the trap set, he came whizzing into the room, and I came up out of that cubical. I'd never heard a man scream before. He leaped flat-footed all the way out into the hallway, and when the ruse was revealed, had to sit down and become calm before he could laugh.

The fun was infectious as the resident came back from lunch early and asked to borrow the costume. After the waiting room had several people standing, waiting to sign in, he announced in a somewhat loud, deep voice, "Tell the doctor I have a rash."

The waiting patients turned to see who this could be and parted as the Red Sea before Moses. All present enjoyed the occasion. That last patient of the morning came back over the years for occasional visits and never failed to mention hearing the male scream upon his visit that memorable Halloween.

GIFTS AND GIVING

A LIFE-CHANGING GIFT

As part of the Christmas Eve Service 1999, our pastor asked four individuals to each speak briefly on the subjects of *lights*, *music*, *gifts*, and a fourth subject, which, regrettably, I have forgotten. I was assigned *gifts* as my topic, and my remarks were mainly the telling of this story about a gift I received and the giver, whom I met when I was about ten years of age, who forever changed my life.

First, I would remind you that when the subject of food appears, most folks mention steak, seafood, or other meat items. But in Alabama where I grew up, often, fried okra, black-eyed peas, cornbread, and sweet potatoes are the subject of conversation when food is mentioned. Can you believe that when I was a teenager working at a drugstore soda fountain, one of the featured flavors of ice cream was sweet potato, called *alayam*?

In late October on a Sunday afternoon, I was invited to go to the country with my friend Staley also aged ten with his uncle and aunt who were rearing him. So off we went in a Model B Ford, not Model T or Model A, which was at least fifteen years old and had a horn that went something like this, *ah-oooo-gah*. We were off the paved roads before we were out of the Auburn city limits, then on gravel, then on dirt, and finally up a narrow lane to an isolated cabin, more aptly and truthfully called a shack, situated in the center of a clearing. The house had one room, no plumbing, electricity, stove, or heating except a fireplace. A pile of rocks supported each corner of the house. There was no porch, and with one step, one was inside the house, three or four of which would fit into our youth assembly room.

As Mr. Fincher conducted his business away from the car with the man of the house, a black man, the other three of us sat in the car and the lady of the house, an old woman of about thirty (everyone over twenty is old to a ten year old) barefoot, and wearing a clean, but much faded and patched dress came to the car bringing each of us a freshly baked sweet potato, served on a scrap of brown grocery sack paper. The potato had, no doubt, been baked in the ashes on the hearth, as we blew these away in order to get inside the skin. Without any utensils, butter or any thing else, we devoured this wonderful food with the thick, sweet, sticky juice getting on our faces and hands.

I noticed her hands, worn from hard work, with many scrapes and abrasions and appearing older than her years. Most of all, I noticed her pleasant countenance, gracious demeanor, and a beautiful smile that emanated, not just from her lips, but from her eyes, and heart as well. I marveled at this black Madonna, who living in the midst of grinding poverty at the height of our national and international depression, and with the barest of essentials, had prepared and served us with a repast fit for a king, still fondly remembered by this Alabama boy as the best prepared and most graciously served sweet potato ever! Her bearing, although illiterate and presumed ignorant, transcended the barriers of race, education, and socio-economic standing.

Only years later, did I realize that she may well have served us their only food, this having been prepared for their supper. I thank her again for this gift and her act of sacrificial giving.

Acts 3:6 says it best: "Silver and gold have I none, such as I have give I thee!"

About four years later, I had a paper route delivering the *Opelika Daily News* called by the locals *Opelika Daily Snooze.* One summer day, I saw an extremely elderly black man sitting on a stone wall near Carter's Grocery on North Gay Street. He was wearing bib overalls with patches sewn on patches, and I noticed his toes protruding from ill-fitting shoes. As I recall, he seemed alone and dejected, apparently just waiting, for what, I did not know, and I felt compassion for him. I parked my bike, went into the store and purchased for him a package of cinnamon rolls and a soft drink. I walked up to where he sat, and in complete reversal of what I had learned in the previous story from the gracious lady, I thrust the food into his hands and without a word jumped on my bike and rode away. Now, who is the ignorant person in these two stories?

I might add Our Father has given me many more opportunities over the years, and I have done better.

FATHER/MOTHER–A TRIBUTE

I could not, in good conscience, write a book without giving tribute to the two people who set me on the path that led to the adventures and experiences related in these writings. They, not only were responsible for my existence, they were the guiding force in molding my values, my outlook, and my early life. They instilled in me a love of my fellowman and a love for my heavenly Father, which have stood me in good stead all through my life.

I wish to acquaint the reader with my parents by giving a glimpse into some of my funniest and fondest memories of my mother and my father.

This tribute to my mother was written as a part of a family history album presented to my children Christmas of 1999, while part of this tribute to my father was written and presented as a children's sermon given at Midway Baptist Church on Father's Day, June 19, 1994.

MEMORIES OF MOTHER

My mother never quite lost her sense of humor even during her protracted illness and death at age 89. She enjoyed telling about this conversation she overheard at the Lee County Hospital, Opelika, Alabama.

Orderly to elderly male patient in room across the hall: "Is you had your enema yet?"

Arab, Alabama School, 1913

Row one, (l to r): Dimple Marsh, Glenn's aunt–his father's sister; (?); (?); (?); (?); Ethel Hanson; ? Barnard–daughter of Robert Barnard; (?); Irene Hinds–daughter of Dr. Will T. Hinds & also Leon Marsh's first grade teacher; (?); Dr. Smith, teacher; Row two: Elzera Wright–daughter of John and Mollie Wright, married Tom Roberts; (?); Alda Camp–daughter of cousin Lewis and Delia Camp, married Bill Johnson; (?); (?); (?); ? Barnard–another daughter of Robert Barnard; (?); (?); Wade Wright–cousin of Joe Wright; Row Three: (?); Ruby Thompson–daughter of Jim and Tempie Thompson, married Claude Eidson; (?); ? Wright–daughter of Thomas Wright; Seaborn Camp–son of Jesse & Hattie Camp; Fannie Linn–daughter of Will Linn, married Dr. J. M. Crawford;(?); (?); Annie Mae Linn–daughter of John and Alice Linn, married Elmer Clotfelter; (?); Joe Wright–son of John and Mollie Wright, & one of Glenn's favorite uncles; Row Four: Ethel Lee Cox (Marsh)–Glenn's mother; A. G. (Albert) Marsh–Glenn's father; (?); (?); (?); (?); (?); Fred Marsh–Glenn's uncle; (?); Frank Lassetter–brother of Uncle Jason Lasseter who was married to Aunt Ella Cox (sister of Ethel Lee); Tom Wright–son of John and Mollie Wright and brother of Joe Wright (Incidentally, this is the Tom Wright who ran over the mailbox and died of pneumonia the next day.)

Patient slowly answering orderly: "I don't know whether I is or whether I ain't."

Orderly responding quickly: "You ain't."

MOTHER'S RELUCTANCE TO ADMIT A MISTAKE

While I believe my mother to be a wonderful person, she had a personality trait that was obvious to us in the family. She didn't like to admit a mistake. I think all people are that way to varying degrees, but she had a "good dose" of it.

Mother's false teeth, now called dentures, had been bothering her for some time, and instead of returning to Dr. Tatum in Opelika, Alabama, she decided to see another dentist, whose name I have long forgotten. (He charged less.) Well, it didn't work out. She liked the new teeth even less than the old ones, so after a few return visits that didn't improve the fit, she gave up and returned to Dr. Tatum, and she was pleased with her new "choppers," but not happy with having to pay twice, and certainly not pleased with having to see the tangible evidence, the visible reminder of her mistake. So one day having again seen these unused and still new teeth on the shelf, she hied herself into that part of the garden farthest from the house and buried her mistake. Well, the years rolled by, my father was no longer able to tend the garden and some time later died. More time elapsed, and even after my father's death, my mother retained their rental house with the garden site, now unused, situated between the two houses.

All tenants, as I remember, were young married students at Auburn University and had at least two traits in common – not much money and the desire to cause the funds they had to stretch further. The tenant husband, at that time, decided a garden was the answer, and so applied to my mother to spade the garden. She agreed and you have already guessed what happened. He dug up the teeth, and thinking he had dug up the skeletal remains of an Indian grave, he excitedly brought his find to my mother.

Albert G. and Ethel Lee Marsh, Glenn's parents, Auburn, Alabama, 1959. My father died the following year. Photo courtesy of Dr. Leon Marsh

She listened respectfully to his blow-by-blow account of his "discovery," but never told him any differently nor acknowledged the ownership of the teeth.

Mother's Ingenuity

We had a '39 Dodge two door sedan, used, that cost $1015. It was OK, ran well, but had one serious drawback. The roof leaked badly. Several tried, but no one seemed to be able to stop this leak.

In my mind's eye, I can see us, in that Dodge traveling down those somewhat narrow two-lane roads. I was ten or eleven years old and riding in the back seat. Daddy was driving. Mother was sitting in the passenger seat with her umbrella opened, keeping dry as we rode in the rain.

MOTHER'S WINNING PERSONALITY

One day at the office, as I was preparing to do some minor surgery on a patient I had seen but once or twice before, this patient remarked how she really missed my mother, who had died but a few months previously. Since this lady lived in Lexington and my mother, at her advanced age, could not have seen or known this lady without my having been present, I asked her how she knew my mother. She replied, "That was the strangest thing. One night she was trying to call you and got my number by mistake. She continued talking and over a period of time and routine calls, we became good friends by telephone."

Mother had never told me of "this mistake" and this, one of the most pleasant surprises, has become one of my favorite memories.

FATHER'S LOVE
A CHILDREN'S SERMON

As we honor our fathers today, I wish to tell you something about my father and my growing up in Alabama. Alabama is a Deep South state, and when I was your age, we were in the midst of a deep worldwide economic depression. Ask your grandparents or great-grandparents about that, but it basically means that almost all the people in the whole country were in want to some extent and thus, were poor as there were few jobs and many people were out of work. All the people I knew were poor, and some did not have enough to eat especially in the larger cities where there were bread lines and soup kitchens established as an attempt to meet people's needs. Kids went to school barefoot until frost, and in a photograph, discovered some years ago, of my first grade class, most of the girls and all the boys are barefoot, including the mayor's son who, otherwise, was decked out in a white linen suit with white shirt and neck-tie. The poorest people did not have flour for making bread, and this dividing line became the title of a book, *But We Didn't Have Cornbread for Breakfast*, meaning one was the very poorest when cornbread had to be substituted for wheat bread at break-fast.

Incidentally, I had two brothers, no sisters and we lived on a farm without electricity or running water, and my mother cooked on a wood-burning stove. A characteristic of people from Alabama is that they use r's in three key words – winder, tomater, and Chicargo.

When son David, who honors me by coming from Florida for Father's Day, was five or six years of age, he asked what channel on TV I watched when his age. I replied, "Television hadn't been invented." He then asked what station I listened to on the radio and I replied, "We had no radio, and even if we had had one, we had no electricity." With widely opened eyes and an expression of amazement, he asked, "Golleeee, were your parents pioneers?"

The family deemed my oldest brother, Ralph, resourceful. His teachers used other, not-so-complimentary words. When electricity was coming in, and workmen set a power pole near the house, he couldn't wait, so tying a string to a rock, he threw this over the lower of the two power lines. He repeated this with the rock and string passing over the top wire, and tying the string to wires, pulled them over the power lines. When he connected the other ends to the borrowed radio, we were able to hear the Grand Ole Opry for free.

This is the same brother who years later, when living in Mississippi, hitched a ride home at Christmas with a student pilot not authorized to transport passengers. He boarded the airplane by running from the woods at the end of the runway, and out of sight of the operations office. Navigation was done by swooping down to read road signs, which were much smaller on the two-lane roads years before today's interstate highways.

With that prolonged background, let me tell you about my father. It was a Saturday in springtime fifty-seven years ago. How do I know that? Well, I was home from school and Daddy kept the Sabbath, not working on Sunday. I was in the second grade and thus, I was seven years old.

Mother told me to take water to my father who was plowing – not with a tractor, as no one in our county had tractors in those days, but with two mules pulling a hand-guided turning plow. He was about from here to the Midway railroad tracks (1/3 mile) or maybe the Corner Grocery (1/2 mile) away. I went to the well. What's that? Simply put, it is a deep hole in the ground with a person on the top of the hole, and if you are lucky, water at the bottom. One gets the water out by letting down a bucket with a rope attached, one end to the bucket and the other to a windlass with a crank that winds the rope and pulls up the bucket. The water is then poured from the bucket to a suitable container, which, on this day, was a glass gallon jug with a ring in the neck where a short rope was attached to serve as a handle. This done, I could "light out" – that's the way we expressed it in those days – across the field.

As I made my way across the field, it was great fun to step on the freshly turned earth, warm on the outside and cool in the inside of the soft clods. Can you imagine a kid in today's world, used to Nintendo, enjoying such a simple pleasure, and those that did wouldn't talk about it. I soon discovered by raising my toes, I could kick the soft loam with the ball of my foot and send a shower of dirt ahead of me. I further discovered that by swinging my water jug, I could send a tremendous shower of dirt ahead of me. By then, my father had seen me coming from a great way off, and stopped so that my course would intercept his position. When I came near, I noticed his tattered straw-hat, much faded blue work shirt, bib overalls, threadbare at the knees, and brogan shoes. Being wet with sweat, the shirt appeared much darker than it really was. He pulled out a ragged red bandanna, and after wiping his face on his sleeve used the bandanna to wipe the inside of the hat sweat band, then wiped his face and neck as he leaned on the plow handles and licked his parched lips as I approached.

When I was about as far away as the wall there (15–20 feet), I took one last sling with the jug at a large mound of dirt. I shouldn't have done that. To my dismay, it wasn't really dirt, but a dirt-covered rock. The glass jug shattered, and the water disappeared immediately into the soft earth. With realization of what I had carelessly done, and seeing the shadow of disappointment, but not anger, cross his face, I burst into tears. He held out his arms, and as I ran into them, he said, "That's all right, son; that's all right." I don't remember to this day what happened to the broken glass in the field, or whether I brought more water, but I do remember thinking in childlike faith that this must be what God is like. My father died in 1960, and my memory of this experience is still vivid after fifty-eight years.

In a perfect world, all of us would have our fathers here today, perhaps, our grandfathers here, but this is not a perfect world and that is not possible. My father died a week before David was born, so David did not get to know his grandfather. In a moment, when you return to your pew, hug and kiss your father. If it is not possible for your father to be here, hug and kiss that responsible person who brought you today.

Happy Father's Day.

MY FATHER'S JOKES

My father was not noted for joke telling, and as I remember, did not have a lengthy repertoire. He is remembered better for liking humorous family stories. However, these two jokes he told, I remember well.

A lady called her local police station with a complaint concerning a large animal in her garden. In fact, she stated, not having seen an elephant before, that it was the largest animal she had ever seen and that part of the garden not trampled was laid waste by the animal's pulling up the vegetables with his tail. The incredulous officer then asked what the animal was doing with the vegetables after they had been pulled up by the animal's tail. The lady replied, "Officer, you would not believe me, if I told you."

Another story concerned three moles, poppa mole, mamma mole, followed by baby mole as they made their way through the soft earth. Poppa mole stopped, saying, "I believe I smell country ham."

Mamma mole said, "I believe I smell pancakes with butter and maple syrup."

Baby mole said, "All I smell is Molasses."

WHAT DID HE EXPECT?

When my father was a young man, he discovered that a friend of his had never had ice cream. My father invited him into a drugstore and ordered two dishes of vanilla ice cream. When both had finished, Daddy asked the stranger to ice cream, "Well, how did you like it?"

"Pretty good," was the reply, "but most of mine was all froze."

DADDY AND THE BIRMINGHAM COP

When a young man and driving in the city of Birmingham, Alabama, my father turned the wrong way and, as a result, was going the wrong way on a one-way street. He was pulled over by the big city officer of the law, asked whence he had come, and when told from Arab, Alabama, the policeman asked, making fun of this hamlet, without a single traffic light, "What do you do with a person in Arab going the wrong way on a one-way street?"

My father replied quickly, "We send them to Birmingham and make cops out of them." With a gusty laugh at his expense, this policeman sent my daddy on his way.

The Shortest Pencil

Glenn; his mother and father, Mr. & Mrs. A. G. (Ethel Lee) Marsh; his brother, Leon; and his brother Ralph (in front). Photo made at East Glenn Ave. in Auburn, Alabama, 1959. Last complete family photo. Father died in 1960 and Ralph died in 1965

Tire Change

In those days of dirt and chert roads and tires that were very susceptible to puncture, a trip of any distance would ordinarily require use of the spare tire. When on the way back to Auburn after visiting relatives in Arab, we had gone less than twelve miles, when the first flat occurred. There was no option but to have the tire or tube repaired, as we had but one spare tire. Stopping in Guntersville, Daddy had a mechanic dismount the tire, patch the tube, reinstall the tube, inflate it, and re-mount the tire. As the wheel was being mounted on the car, the mechanic installed a single lug nut, then without installing the other lug nuts, and semi-tightening them in the usual way, he applied full force to the lug wrench, resulting in a screech of metal against metal as the lug reached bottom.

My father had seen enough, and in a reasonable tone said, "I'd rather you install all the lugs, finger-tighten them, then wrench-tighten them in opposing fashion."

The workman objected, and in a most vociferous tone informed my father saying, "I've worked here all of my life, and this is the way I've always done it."

My father replied dryly, "That may be so, but I'd think you'd have to be at least seven or eight years old to be of much help around here."

No blows were exchanged, but it was close.

By the Sweat of Your Brow

It gets hot in Alabama in the summertime, and in the early 1940s when my father was working as a mechanic at the Tillage Machinery Laboratory, he was dripping wet with sweat – not a dry thread in his clothing, and had found a resting place to catch his breath. Mr. I. F. Reed, the head of this facility, ran a very tight ship. Seeing my father sitting down, he inquired with a hint of disappointment in his voice, "Mr. Marsh, what are you doing?"

My father replied, "Restin' and when I get done with that, I'm goin' to have a Co-cola [*Alabamaese* for Coca-Cola]." Mr. Reed, who never laughed and seldom smiled, grunted his acknowledgment and passed by.

In 1998 at the Auburn High School reunion, I told Mary Jo, Mr. Reed's daughter this story; she related that she had seen her father smile infrequently, but never laugh.

THE VISITOR

One of my all-time favorite stories comes to me from my father who witnessed the drama.

This occurred during the war years (WW II) and involved a co-worker at this same Tillage Machinery Laboratory. The co-worker was Mr. Ed Hansen, a machinist of exceptional ability and of German extraction. One day a workman yelled across the shop saying, "Ed, there's someone here to see you."

Ed yelled back, "Yeh, who is it?"

The reply, "I don't know. He says he's your brother." With doubt clearly on his face, Mr. Hansen made his way to the door, opened it, and the most amazing scene of his life confronted him. There stood a US Army truck, with armed guards, the truck loaded with German prisoners of war, except one, standing on the ground, waiting to see his brother, the machinist.

I leave it to the reader's imagination to recreate this reunion of brothers.

I have reflected many times about the risk taken by someone, a hero in my opinion, redirecting these prisoners so that one might see his brother.

Humanity in action!

ENTERING THE WORLD OF WORK

The Lipscomb Connection

After having worked at the busiest drugstore in Auburn, it was much better for me at Lipscomb's Drugstore, also known interchangeably as Tiger Drugs (there was a tiger everything in Auburn using the mascot of the athletic teams of A.P.I.) and as the Rexall Store, the outlet for that brand in Auburn. I had long since learned all there was to know about the soda fountain at the busy drugstore. Now, I could do other things including waiting on customers buying over-the-counter remedies as well as all those items that made up drugstore merchandise in those days (guitar strings, pinochle cards, candles, cosmetics). Mr. A. D. "Lan" Lipscomb, who was affectionately known far and wide as "Dr. Lan," was the owner, a kindly man, honest, decent in all ways, lover of a good joke, or funny situation, attender of the Georgia Tech-Auburn football game most years, and most of all, sort of a second father to me.

He was of slight stature and an inveterate smoker of Philip Morris cigarettes. Having a shock of gray hair and an inborn trust of people, with a facility for calmness, he was a good teacher. Being one of the first people I'd ever met who recognized that the first step in discipline is instruction, he showed me exactly how he wanted the ice cream cones dipped, the limes cut and squeezed for the limeades, and the prescriptions filled. He knew my pharmacy goals early on and allowed, even welcomed, me into that part of the store in which I was most interested. His

Mr. Andrew D. Lipscomb, owner of Lipscomb's Drug Store, N. College Street, Auburn, Alabama. Dr. Lan as he was affectionately known far and wide was my mentor during the impressionable teenage years and along with my father was the male role-model whom I admired and emulated. His influence on my life is inestimable. Photo circa 1940, courtesy Carolyn Ellis Lipscomb

prescription charges were modest and his temper, if he had one, was subdued. I ought to know, as I was responsible through poor penmanship for a 300 block of unused prescription numbers. My poor penmanship has been a joke and a cause for embarrassment for me all of my life. [I even received poor grades for penmanship in grammar school.] You see, my fours look like sevens which accounts for the above mistake, and not learning from this experience, I was doomed to repeat this mistake years later when I was asked to write some letters encouraging the attendance of some scattered friends at the wedding of our mutual friend, the groom. The guests came all right, at seven in the evening, rather than at four, the actual time of the wedding. It took a long time to live that down.

As was Dr. Lan, Mrs. Lipscomb was always nice to me, but, of course, seeing her on a rather infrequent basis, I did not ever establish a relationship beyond that of wife of the boss and my employer. Mrs. Lipscomb (Freddie) was the daughter of Dr. I.S. McAdory, dean of the School of Veterinary Medicine. Dr. McAdory somewhere or other had heard that I was active in church and made a point of expressing his approval especially after he heard that I helped with the offering. This was a pleasant, much appreciated observation and made an impression on this teenager – this is one of those seemingly insignificant events, especially to the one making the overture, but of great importance to the recipient.

Dr. Lan's son, referred to as Lan Jr., was overseas during WW II in Europe during much of the time I worked at the drugstore. I thought him much more like his dad than his brother, Mac. Lan Jr. and I hit it off well from the beginning and I liked listening to his "war stories" which were to me, as a history buff, fascinating. Most were humorous reflecting his father's love of a funny story, such as taking an **empty** hot water bottle to bed with him at night. Why? Well, it was a long way to the outside latrine especially on a cold winter's night. He also related making a long slit in each side of his G.I. sleeping bag. This way, if the Germans overran the Army position, he could stick his feet and legs through, one on each side, pull the sleeping bag up like a giant diaper and run to the rear area to safety.

I did not know Mac nearly so well for some reason or other. He became owner of Toomer's Drugstore, on Toomer's Corner, also known by virtue of sports broadcasts where it is publicized both for its historic role in Auburn life and for its lemonade. I've never had a lemonade there, though son Franky gave them top rating.

Sadly, Mac and Lan Jr. both died the same year. I read of their deaths in the *Auburn Pharmacist* and as a result re-established contact with Carolyn Ellis Lipscomb, Lan Jr.'s widow and a school chum of mine, whom I remembered from Mrs. Lane's second grade class, as having held up her hand to get permission to go to the water fountain.

When Mrs. Lane inquired, "What do you want, Carolyn?" she stated, "I want to get a drink of wahtahr" Interestingly, Carolyn has never lost that beautiful deep Alabama accent, and can, on occasion, get about as many syllables as letters in a word.

Speaking of pronunciation, Dr. Lan pronounced my name Glan, rhyming with "Lan," and I liked to imagine that I reminded him of his son Lan, away in Europe. Dr. Lan was a fair and equitable employer. In those early days the pay was thirty cents per hour. A five cent Hershey bar was long enough to stick out of one's pocket, Kotex was twenty-seven cents per box, and toilet paper, three rolls for a quarter. Once when Dr. Lan and his family took an infrequent vacation to Florida, and the other pharmacist was incapacitated by his affinity for the contents of the "bottle," I appointed myself as pharmacist and took on the responsibility of the store. When a doctor would call in a prescription and wish to speak to the pharmacist, I would say, "Just a moment," lay down the phone, pick it up again and in the deepest voice I could muster say, "Good afternoon, doctor, may I help you?" After he gave me the prescription, I would fill it and on occasion, deliver it. When the Lipscombs returned, Dr.

Lan was most appreciative of my efforts on his behalf and raised my pay to thirty-five cents per hour and showed even more interest in teaching me the art and practice of pharmacy. When he and I worked together, he allowed me to drive his '37 Packard [or was it a Buick?] coupe to make prescription deliveries rather than use my bicycle. That was a special treat, and that coupe with its straight eight engine made a long, lean vehicular package, and in my eyes, if only for the twenty minutes it took to go to any point in Auburn and return to the drugstore, I (at 16 years old) was a man about town.

Somewhere about that time, money began missing from the cash register receipts. The main cash register in the pharmacy part of the store was a great big outfit with a lever that had to be turned to ring up the sale. [It would bring a small fortune at an antique sale these days.] This was a bad time for the employees as well as for the owner. No one was comfortable and the situation was worsened by the decision to allow only designated employees (I was one) ring up sales. A break in the case came when I was working up front in the store alone, except for the delivery boy. I needed something from the back, and as I walked fast in those days, and hastily neared the rear of the store where the office and safe were, I heard the distinct sound of the safe's closing. Seconds later said-delivery boy came around the corner toward me, the picture of innocence, too innocent. I told Dr. Lan. The delivery boy was fired, and there were no more thefts that I know of. Dr. Lan was a most trusting employer. Hayward Reed, my best friend, also worked there, and one day I said to him, "Dr. Lan sure does trust people." Hayward replied with marvelous insight, "Honest people trust other people."

I believe that is an original thought, and I thank Hayward for this bit of insight and wisdom. I was reminded of this as recently as 1998, at the time of our high school reunion. After not having seen Hayward for many years, we found ourselves checking into the motel at the same time. How appropriate since our friendship was a local legend. Some joking teachers and

Judy, Glenn, and Hayward Reed, my best friend of pre-college days. Picture taken in front of Auburn Grille, 1998.

friends called us the David and Jonathan of Lee County High School, and they were right. Someone asked me later what was it like seeing Hayward again after all those years. I said, "It's about like having last seen him in May when school was out, and now it is September, and school was in again."

The next morning having breakfast at the Auburn Grille, Hayward remarked how many of our classmates were dead and how so many seemed to be in poor health. He wondered why. I reminded him since we had seen each other, there had been a constant stream of banter with much laughter and camaraderie just like the "good old days." I feel that laughter and attitude have much to do with one's outlook.

To quote Irving Berlin: "Life is five percent what one makes of it and ninety-five percent how one takes it."

With my attendance at the Lee County High School reunion and with my renewed friendship with Carolyn Lipscomb and others from my high school days, memories of growing up in Auburn surfaced. The following vignettes are some of those notable, humorous, and pleasant memories of the Lipscomb connection:

DELIVERY BOY

The phone number at Lipscomb's Drugstore was 200 in those days, and it was not infrequent that someone wishing the president of API would reply "200" in answer to the telephone operator's "Number, please." Dr. Duncan's extension number was also 200, so when one failed, to go, first through the college switch board, to ask for the extension, and instead just asked for 200, the person would get NUMBER 200 rather than EXTENSION 200. On occasion when this would occur, and Dr. Lan was feeling somewhat mischievous, he would tell the caller that Dr. Duncan was out on delivery and would be back in a matter of a few minutes or half-hour or whatever. This was a sort of an in-house joke, and when this event would occur, we would laugh as if it were the very first time. I wonder if Dr. Duncan ever knew that he was referred to as a delivery boy.

DR. LAN'S ADVICE

Dr. Lan, as I have noted, was very kind to me, and I can think of not a single person to whom he was unkind. I sensed he truly liked me. He often gave me various bits and pieces of advice, and on occasion, his tips surprised me. Once he said, "Glan, when you get married and have children and the baby cries on a cold winter night, I've found that if you slip your foot out from under the cover, let it cool, and carefully ease it back under the cover up against your wife's back, she'll wake up saying, "I hear the baby fussing; I'm going to fix a bottle."

I never knew, in times like these, whether he was serious or putting me on. Makes no difference, just a fond, humorous memory.

Caroline Lipscomb and Lan; granddaughter and son of Mr. A. D. Lipscomb. Caroline is a pharmacist also, thus the third generation Lipscomb pharmacist. Caroline is the daughter of Lan and Carolyn Ellis Lipscomb. Photo 1979, courtesy of Carolyn Ellis Lipscomb

MAH-REE!

One day when Lan Jr. had walked down to "the Greeks" [that was the way many people referred to the Gazes brothers who owned the Auburn Grille] for coffee, an apparently young lady called, referred to herself as Marie, but pronounced the name "Mah-ree," and in a rather breathless, if not urgent way, asked to speak to Lan Jr.

Dr. Lan explained that Lan was not there, but would return shortly and could Lan return the call. "On, no," she said somewhat firmly, indicating that she would call back.

So she did, the next day, again while Lan Jr. was out for coffee. If anything, she seemed a bit more anxious to talk with Lan Jr., but again, would not leave her number. When Dr. Lan asked Lan Jr. about the calls, he protested that he knew no one of that name.

The third call came in, as before, and the lady seemed close to panic when she missed Lan Jr. again. Dr. Lan cornered his son and said something on the order of, "Son, who is the woman? Is there something you need to tell me? I'm your father."

Lan Jr. was somewhat indignant at his father's inference saying, "Daddy, you know me better than that. I'd never do anything."

Seems that John C. Ball Jr. and his wife had noted from their furniture store across College Street, the comings and goings of Lan 1 and Lan 2 and had planned, and executed the whole scenario. That's the way Auburn folks had fun before TV.

It's For All of Us

Lipscomb's Drugstore was long and narrow, as were most of the stores of that era. There was, near the pharmacy part of the store, a wrapping counter adjacent to the giant cash register, and this counter was the repository for the *charge book*, a long, heavy account book wherein was entered the charges for customers not paying cash.

Dr. Lan knew nearly everyone in Auburn with his recognition extending to his or her children. One day, however, an unknown youngster came in to purchase toilet paper. Dr. Lan waited on him, bagged, and handed him the merchandise. As the kid headed toward the front door, Dr. Lan, not recognizing the young man, and thus, not knowing to whom the purchase should be charged, called out to him, "Son, who is this for?" Without breaking stride, the young man called back, "It's for all of us."

In memory, I see Dr. Lan draped over that charge book, arms extended, having the laugh of the week, if not of the month. He made no further attempt to establish the identity. The laugh was payment enough.

Phono Vision

When I was a senior at Lee County High School, now Auburn High School, I had worked part time at Lipscomb's Drugstore for several years. At this time, one of my classmates, R. W., came to work and surprisingly, he had never before used the telephone. For the first few days, he avoided the phone like the plague, but once he began using it, he would literally run over the other employees to get to the phone first.

One day, when involved in a phone conversation with a customer, and there was some difficulty in explaining the various sizes, i.e. contents and prices, involved in a certain item, I heard him say to the customer, "Just a minute, ma'am, and I'll get the sizes we have and show you."

"Send Him a Dozen"

One night, a customer phoned the drugstore and another pharmacist (B. S.) took the call. He understood that the customer wanted three-dozen condoms to be delivered. The pharmacist, thinking this in error, asked that he repeat the order. Again, it sounded like "three dozen" were being requested. Somewhat apprehensive about asking the customer to repeat his order a third time, he asked Dr. Lan what he should do.

Dr. Lan said, "Send him a dozen. That'll get him through the night."

POTPOURRI

The following vignettes are a collection of random experiences that do not fit into the other categories, but which, I hope, the reader might find interesting as they present a mix of human interest.

DOUBTING THOMASES

In my office, I would frequently encounter patients who seemed to require a definite reason for the medical event that brought them to see me. There were a few who still thought that a black cat crossing the road ahead of them – but significant only if crossing from left to right – was the cause of their misfortune. Others insisted that the cause was because of some aberration of their "system" whatever that is, while others would have arrived at an irrational, bizarre cause and effect, which resisted my best efforts at dissuading them of their erroneous conclusion. For this group, I resorted to the absurd by telling them truthfully that I had a garden and that since I had erected scarecrows that I had had no problem at all with elephants trampling my garden. This was a lesson in cause and effect that illustrated how the wrong conclusions can be drawn from irrelevant information.

For those who continued to insist with the question, "Why me?" I resorted to a personal account of infectious disease experience in the army at Fort Chaffee, Arkansas in December 1950 and January 1951.

During basic training, my 220 man Company A, 81st Medium Tank Battalion wore the same clothing, i. e. uniform, ate the same food in the army mess hall, had the same activity prescribed by duty schedule, and the same amount of rest with lights out at 9:00 p. m.

Almost all had colds, but not all; a few had pneumonia, and only one or two had meningitis. Why did we not all have the same medical disorders? I would ascertain the reason to be individual susceptibility, or looked at another way, individual resistance. In this instance, we had little or nothing to do with the cause of our illnesses, in so far as our own actions were concerned. I am persuaded that in life, bad things can and do happen to good people and vice versa. It does indeed, rain on the just and the unjust.

However, B. A. Campbell, an elderly friend of mine from Texas used to say of me, "Doc, you have more ideas than anyone I've ever known, and not a one of them worth a damn."

There are Moles and There are "Moles"

One day in the office, I saw an attractive lady who was wearing quite distinctive apparel. The lacy blouse had, for instance, sleeves almost totally covering the backs of her hands. The collar came up to jawbone-level and was buttoned above the base of her neck. She wanted advice relative to her "moles."

Upon exam, they weren't moles at all, but represented an attempt to create moles with very poor results. They were bizarre in color and configuration, and while none were really mole like, there were several noticeable scars, resulting from inept attempts at removal of those considered not acceptable.

It seems her husband was "turned on" by moles, and since she didn't have enough of the "real McCoy" to satisfy him, he had tried to fabricate others. I felt quite sorry for her and suggested a cessation of the *home cookin'* of moles, and an evaluation by a plastic surgeon. I guess I should have also recommended a psychiatrist. I never saw her again.

HAIRY FINGERPRINT

While in the service, I saw a dentist who had a hairy thumb pad. He was injured in a childhood accident resulting in loss of significant tissue from this area. Skin for a graft was taken from a usually non-hairy area, and upon his reaching adulthood, hair did surprisingly grow from this skin graft. Therefore, each morning, he shaved his thumb prior to going to the office.

THE THREE MOST OVERRATED THINGS
IN THE WORLD

While Emory University School of Medicine was, and still is, a top medical and medical education facility, every now and then there would appear to be, at least, a vestige of professional envy, and the most common verbalization of this was, "The three most overrated things in the world are home cooking, sex, and the Mayo Clinic."

The only personal application of this came to me in the first few months after opening my medical practice. A female patient came from Harrodsburg, Kentucky about thirty-five miles away, and according to her medical history, she had had her baffling dermatologic condition for a few years. With failure on the local scene as to diagnosis and treatment, she then traveled to Rochester, Minnesota to the Mayo Clinic. After several days there and a sizable bill of about $10,000 (in the late 1960s), she came home without diagnosis or effective treatment.

She then, heard about the new dermatologist in Lexington and decided to try me. As unbelievable as it may seem, I recognized her problem, explained the diagnosis, and started her on appropriate medication. The medication required close monitoring of dosage because of potentially serious side effects. She responded promptly and without side effects. The dosage was reduced twice, and she was dismissed after about three visits, but warned that while she was under control, flare-ups usually occurred after some time interval, and when and if, this occurred, she would need to return for adjusting of dosage as determined by her condition.

About a year or so later, she called, having experienced the predicted flare-up, and when told by the nurse that she would need an appointment so that the doctor could determine the increased dosage to be prescribed, depending upon the severity of her condition, she had another "flare-up," exclaiming angrily, "I'm not coming all the way to Lexington and paying $8 for an office visit for a refill."

No one suggested the Mayo Clinic as an alternative.

DEMOGRAPHICS AND GEOGRAPHICS

Interestingly, patients came to me for acne management from farther away than for other problems, with quite a few also traveling quite a distance for their shingles treatment.

We kept a map on the wall in the hallway of the office and used pins to mark the cities whence patients came. In the East as far away as West Virginia, and Virginia (very few), and the North from Ohio (occasionally), South from Tennessee, but can't think of any from Missouri. On the eastern half of Kentucky, actually, from a point about half way from Lexington to Elizabethtown to the Kentucky-West Virginia-Virginia border, the map was a thicket of pins. I remember one humorous event relative to this.

It was a quite snowy day in Lexington with little traffic; snow had fallen most of the previous night. We had seen but two or three patients when I heard a patient come in from Ohio, apologizing for being an hour late. No matter. I happened to be looking out an examining room window at this time at the snow and saw the house about a hundred and fifty yards whence we had already received a cancellation call as the weather was "just too bad" to get out.

TARGET SHOOTING AND HUNTING

A lifelong interest in shooting has brought me in contact with some wonderful friends and delightful experiences over the years.

While model airplanes were far and away, my chief interest during the teen years, I also did some hunting. Inasmuch as I had no gun, this endeavor was not easily accomplished. My oldest brother would always include me when I visited him in Mississippi. Sometimes at Thanksgiving, I would borrow a .22 rifle and hunt on Mr. Robert Hudson's farm, now the location of the Auburn University Veterinary Medicine School, on Wire Road or Mr. Felton Little's farm, south of Auburn which was an interesting place, as there was an abandoned covered bridge there. I can't remember taking any game at either place.

However, this limited exposure to guns and hunting gave me a start, and so in Army basic training, I did well, ranking as expert with the service rifle. After my Army service, but before re-entry as a medical officer, I was on the Army Reserve Rifle Team. When I arrived at Fitzsimons General Hospital in Denver, as an intern, I became a member of the Denver Muzzleloading Gun Club. Attending my first muzzleloading

US Army Reserve Rifle team. Glenn Marsh, second from right, second row, Atlanta, Georgia, ca. 1960

shoot ever, and characteristic of this group of devotees to this old time sport, a member, now deceased, Lloyd Niemieier, lent me his rifle which was a D. H. Hilliard, under-hammer target rifle, furnished the black powder, caps, and hand-cast round lead balls for this "cap'n ball" rifle. The match was held on Father's Day 1961 at Camp George West near Denver. Surprisingly, of all things, I was the first-place medal winner, beating the owner with the rifle, which he had been so kind to lend me. This medal is treasured in my trophy case to this day.

After leaving Denver, and entering dermatology residency in San Antonio, Texas, I was a member of the Alamo Muzzleloading Gun Club and continued this interest after arriving in Kentucky, shooting well enough to be on the Kentucky Longrifle Team of the Kentucky Corps of Longriflemen and shooting in interstate longrifle competition.

A repeat of the Denver experience occurred when I attended the fall shoot of the George Rogers Clark Muzzleloading Gun Club in Kentucky after moving to Fort Knox.

Mr. J. O. Gilpin lent me his rifle, furnished the powder, caps, and lead bullets, and again, I won the match with a heretofore stranger's gun. This sort of friendly rivalry is more the norm than exception among members shooting the old time guns.

Being one of the commanding general's doctors at Fort Knox, allowed access to this commander and with his permission, I scheduled a competitive match of the longrifle team with the Army Marksmanship Team at that post. In shoulder-to-shoulder competition, matching our primitive flintlock rifles against finely tuned, accurized, military service rifles, we were defeated by only sixteen points out of about nine hundred plus points. Quite an accomplishment! Marksmanship is marksmanship, whatever the chosen instrument, or as someone said, "He who shooteth a flintlock rifle well, shooteth anything well."

CARRELL EAKLE

Over the years spent in Lexington, I have met and utilized the services of many persons including attorneys, accountants, architects, surveyors, realtors, carpenters, roofers, and painters. Some of these professionals and trades persons became very good friends as well as rendering necessary services pertinent to their varied abilities.

The most revered friend/professional in the above group is Carrell Eakle, my accountant of over 30 years. I was one of his first clients and while a "small fish" as clients go, have always received "big fish" attention from the very beginning. I noted with pride the growing-up of his children, one son doing a mini-rotation through my office while a student at Sayre School. I am apprised of the educational progress of his children still at home and take pride in their remarkable and significant honors and their achievements.

Carrell, I started with nothing and with your help, have managed to hold onto most of it.

But seriously, thank you, Carrell, for your sage advice, sympathetic ear, and true friendship.

SPECIAL OCCASIONS

I am not much of a shopper, never have been, and prefer the pages of L. L. Bean, Land's End, and nowadays, Sierra, over any in-person shopping. At the time of this event being related, I did some buying by catalogue from Joseph Banks in Baltimore, especially the 100% cotton boxer style shorts. Noticing my underwear drawer becoming depleted, I ordered from this firm several pairs of this item. A courteous reply stated that this item had been discontinued. On the following Friday evening after work, I made the rounds of several malls, but could find no 100% cotton boxer shorts. In order to save a possible repetition of this search, I asked secretary, Barbara M., and nurse, Sue, that when out shopping, especially looking for clothing items for their husbands, if they would inquire if the previously mentioned unmentionables were stocked at that particular store. Their search was as *fruit of the loomless* as mine.

Several weeks passed and one Saturday the new Joseph Banks catalogue arrived, with the much-sought undies now available again. Voilá!

Early Monday morning, as I was filling out an order for twelve pairs, Sue arrived for work. True to form, she wanted to know what I was ordering, so I informed her that the shorts were again available. She wanted to know what colors were available, and what color I had in mind. As she joined me in looking at the ad, I said, "Sue, all I want is white, plain vanilla." She then said, "Look, they have paisley which would be nice for special occasions."

An opening, at last, and I exploited it saying, "Sue, on special occasions, I don't need underwear of any color." She got out of the order-processing mode in a hurry, making a quick exit down the hall, and I assure the reader that subject never came up again.

Danny Boy

This song is my favorite. I am a collector of instrumental and vocal arrangements of which I have in excess of three dozen. I like almost all of them and about two or three are a full cut above the others. The words from the earliest version [there are many other versions] of this haunting melody are

Oh Danny boy, the pipes, the pipes are calling
From glen to glen, and down the mountainside
The summer's gone, and all the flowers are dying
'Tis you, 'tis you must go and I must bide
Refrain
But come ye back when summer's in the meadow
Or when the valley's hushed and white with snow
'Tis I'll be there in sunshine or in shadow
Oh Danny boy, oh Danny boy, I love you so.

Having progressed through this book to the end and learned something of my nature, did you really think it would end on the above serious note?

Think again.

"I have come to that point in life where I avoid weddings and funerals, especially my own!"   –G. Marsh

Finis

The above figure seen interspersed throughout this book represents one of the primitive (folk) art forms seen not uncommonly as an inlay ornamentation or embellishment on the Kentucky Rifle. This rifle is a true example of a colonial creation or at worst an evolvement of central European hunting arms as adapted to the New World.

This seemingly geometric figure, really an eight-pointed star, was also known to be used on the German *Jaeger* (hunter) rifle, the ancestor of the Kentucky Rifle, and some would say possibly is a representation of the Nativity star. This star, individually fashioned by hand from brass or silver, was located on the cheekpiece of the rifle and varied greatly in form among the works of various gunmakers who used this ornamentation. Some were plain, others engraved, but all reflected a personal touch, and as the reader will observe in the illustration, they were not perfectly shaped or executed.

This star is an artistic feature used on the cheekpiece of very early Kentucky Rifles, as later Kentucky rifles were often ornamented with half or quarter moon representations, with the very latest having no such ornamentation of either kind.

Over the years, the term *Hunter's Star* has become the generally accepted appellation for this star.